Before the Deluge

SEBASTIAN MOORE OSB
and ANSELM HURT OSB

NEWMAN PRESS
New York, N.Y.   Glen Rock, N.J.
Amsterdam   Toronto   London

Published by Newman Press
Editorial Office: 304 W. 58th St., N.Y., N.Y. 10019
Business Office: Glen Rock, N.J. 07452

First published, Geoffrey Chapman Ltd., London, 1968

© 1968 Anselm Hurt and Sebastian Moore

Library of Congress Catalog Card No. 68-57109

Nihil obstat: Very Rev. Dom Leo Smith OSB
Imprimi protest: Rt Rev. Dom Victor Farwell OSB, Abb. Press.
8 March, 1968

Printed in Great Britain

CONTENTS

Part One

Sebastian Moore OSB

Part Two

Anselm Hurt OSB

PART ONE

I

INTRODUCTORY

New wine and new skins

HOW AMAZINGLY *vivid* Christ's teaching is! Christ is bringing us something new. He is announcing the radical and definitive renewal of man in the Spirit of God. Now, we all know how man reacts to a new situation. He tries to fit it into his own way of thinking. He likes novelties, provided he can keep to his own way, the way he has got used to. He doesn't want to be jolted out of that. There are heaps of examples of this. For instance, when new ideas are in the wind, the Establishment seeks to satisfy the revolutionaries by making *adjustments* to its way of running things. The conservative tries to weather the storm by adopting a few of the new ideas and so acquiring the *appearance* of modernity while remaining, basically, set on the old ways. Often one meets people who profess to be all out for the new ideas in the Church, and would be amazed and hurt if one told them that at root, they are still died-in-the-wool reactionaries. One meets priests—and this is also a self-criticism—who profess to believe in consulting the laity, but whose instinctive reaction to healthy personal criticism is still thoroughly clerical. We are ALL die-hards in respect of God's Spirit.

No, really new ideas require a radically new inner mind. Christ knew this well. He knew it better than anyone else. What he was bringing was the newest thing ever, and so it made the maximum demand on the human heart to look at the new ideas with new eyes.

But how did he bring this home to us? He said, 'Look, you've got an old coat with a tear in it. Now, being old, this coat has been shrunk by many washings. Suppose you try to mend the tear by sewing on a patch of *new* material. At the next wash, the new patch will shrink and the old coat won't, so the patch will tear the coat even further.' Or, 'Look, you've got an old wineskin. Don't pour in new wine because the lively new wine will expand and burst the old skin.'

So, he concludes, 'for new wine, then, fresh skins'. And that is his slogan. It bites into the mind with the force of a simple, tangible event, the tearing old cloth, the bursting old skins. And how it speaks to us today!

God and the conservatives

It has recently been said, by an American philosopher, that belief in God and Conservatism tend to go together. This is a vast generalization, but there is just enough truth in it to merit serious attention. Conservatism and Socialism represent the two great human values: of order, tradition, stability; and of challenge, revolution, making things new.

Now I think that historically the Church has lined up far more with stability than with revolution. The Church, after all, created our Western civilization, and civilization means order. And thus the image of God that has predominated is the image of the Monarch, benevolent and loving indeed, but basically the Ruler.

But if this is the predominant image of God, if this is what God is thought to stand for, it follows that people who instinctively think in terms of order and stability will incline towards religion, whereas the revolutionary will tend away from it. For him, God will be part of the establishment which he rejects.

If we examine the Christian revelation, we find it to be, above all, revolutionary. The Christian religion is built not on a hallowed human order committed to a priesthood, but on the body of a man shamefully executed by the established order which he challenged. The God who sponsored this procedure is not a serene monarch in whose name the people are to be kept in order, but a profoundly mysterious being who is encountered by him who gives all for his brethren.

Perhaps it is only in our time that the true Christian image of God is beginning to come through. Today we contemplate the astounding spectacle of nuns—those symbols of obedience and order—joining in anti-racialist demonstrations. And we have recently seen the restarting of the worker-priest movement in France. God is becoming associated with the joining of men in brotherhood rather than with their being ruled. Paternalism is ending, and the mysterious face of the eternal Father is beginning to appear. Man will open his heart to a God who does not 'rule us for our good' but who *is* our good, our gathering into one.

Should we not expect this evolution in Christian man? When St Paul looked forward to our 'coming together into the perfect man, the age and fulness of Christ', he was not referring to a process that remains at square one so long as time lasts and which with the end of time is suddenly brought to completion. He was talking of a real historical process, and who shall deny that we today are at a critical stage of it?

The violence of God's love

Recall the parable in which the king, outraged at the ingratitude of those he had invited, 'destroyed those murderers and burned their city'. Elsewhere and similarly, Christ connects the terrible sack of Jerusalem by the Romans with Jerusalem's

rejection of himself. And again, Simeon foresees that the child
will be 'for the rise and *fall* of many'. Countless parables tell of
rejection for those who do not accept their invitation.

This theme of rejection is embedded in the gospel. If we are
honest, it makes us feel uncomfortable. We don't think much of
people who offer us kindness but 'give us hell' if we don't accept
it. And yet it seems that this is the way God behaves. If we
forget religion for a moment and turn to the current affairs
of men, we see this rejection-principle constantly at work. A
privileged class which holds on to its position, which insists on
maintaining the world as it has known it (whereas the world is
constantly evolving), is doomed. And if it holds on tenaciously
it is violently swept aside. It is surely for this reason, for instance,
that one trembles for the future of Rhodesia.

Now if the gospel is about anything it is about a radical change
in the world: *the* change, *the* painful step forward, *the* painful
rebirth, from the old man to the new. And if this world-
change is real, if it is *the* evolution of which common evolution
is but the hint and the shadow, it is impossible for it not to en-
tail the rejection of those who refuse to read the signs of the
times and prefer to stay in their rut. The floods come, the
rut is washed away and is no longer a perceptible track.

This terrible and wonderful lesson of the gospel is addressed
also to the Church today. She too, we too—nay we especially—
are called upon to read the signs of the times and reject old
and outworn attitudes. For instance, an old priest said to me
in London recently: 'If the Church does not find it in herself,
in her own depths, to foster a new, creative, and outgoing love
between white people and coloured, she will fail the people to
whom God has sent her, and come herself under the sentence
of God.'

II

CHRIST

Redemption

PEOPLE FIND THE DOCTRINE of the redemption difficult, which is a pity because we experience the *need* for redemption several times a day, probably without knowing it.

When you look at the situation in Vietnam and the world situation generally, and are overcome with the impossible complexity of it all, you declare, whether you know it or not, the need for redemption. When you consider your own situation at home or at work and the human problems for which no one seems to be responsible, you declare, whether you know it or not, the need for redemption.

In short, whenever you encounter evil at the point where it is diffused in the human condition without hope of being pinned down and dealt with—and this is the characteristic situation of man—you are learning, whether you know it or not, the mysterious language of the cross. For on the cross God declares himself outrageously just where *we* say nothing can be done, namely in the situation of mortal man that culminates quite logically in murder. You can no more blame any individual for the death of Christ than you can blame any individual for the situation in Vietnam or in your family or at work. In abolishing the death penalty—even for horrific murders—our society is perhaps coming alive to the Christian truth that underlying any crime there is a situation of tragic complexity which neither our justice nor our mercy can touch.

From the crucified, set squarely in the midst of our impossibilities, comes new life. We cannot 'cope', in the ordinary way, with the situation at home or at work or in the world, but we can receive from Christ the mysterious power to suffer it creatively. And it must emphatically be said that situations approached in *that* way do *not* remain unchanged. Let's face it, we are called upon by Christ to quicken the world through dying. It's not easy, but the reward is to feel in yourself, just a little and only from time to time, the power of the resurrection. And that is worth just everything. We should be prepared to pay *any* price for a *real* experience of Christ in the sacraments such as the Church, today especially, seeks. Doubtless we are helped *towards* this by liturgical renewal. But the only way to *have* it is to be fully a man or a woman, to encounter the impossibilities, and to suffer them creatively in the power of *the* Man.

Structure and life

The leading atheist in this country has been quoted as saying: 'The influence of Christianity in the coming years will depend not on what Christians say but on what they do and are.' Twenty centuries back our Lord said: 'By this shall men know that you are my disciples, by the love you have for one another.'

As little as ten years ago, we felt able to distinguish ourselves as Catholics by all sorts of things *other* than the quality of our *lives*. There was the pope, the bishops, and the whole impressive spectacle of a world-wide organization. We belonged to *that*, and that was something to be proud of. If someone produced the word 'catholic' in conversation, the *first* image that arose in the mind was probably a piece of ecclesiastical millinery.

In our days, the picture is dramatically changing. The externals of Catholic life and worship used to hold us *emotionally*. They do so no longer. And when our atheist says that this sort of thing cuts no ice in the world, we are forced to admit that it cuts no ice with us either. We are approaching the point where the only image that will hold us will be that of a crucified carpenter who has identified himself with our neighbour and demands that we accord to our neighbour from the bottom of our heart the title of 'brother'.

Understand me well. A man to whom God has shown his Son in the light of faith will be compelled to attach himself to the visible Church. For that light shows to him not just an *example* of the good life, but *the good life itself* as a historical fact. So the Church must be as historical as Christ was, and a community cannot be historical without being institutional. The structure of the Church is necessary, but it is only the structure, the skeleton. It is not the flesh. The flesh is being crucified all around you: next door and in Vietnam. And it is only by your response to these challenges that you become really, actively, a Christian and a Catholic. If you ignore these demands and try to remain a Catholic, you will be a man embracing a skeleton.

It will be asked: if a man distinguishes himself as a Christian only by his openness to the needs of others, why be a Christian at all? What *is* the 'plus' that Christians are supposed to have? Well, there *is* a very long answer, whose elaboration keeps the religious book industry going. But there's a short answer, and this is the best one: get on with the job and Christ will show you. Get on with the job, and Christ will show you to the world as one of his own.

Corpus Christi

The primitive Church preached Christ our Lord. What then did *Christ* preach? Did he preach himself, was he the first Christian, did he talk about himself? Sometimes, but more basically, he *showed* himself, he made a gesture to people. In responding to that gesture they were conscious of their life as totally renewed: and in this consciousness of renewal they proclaimed Christ as the renewer of all life, as the saviour of the world.

But what was this gesture of Christ, this gesture that Christ was? It was a gesture of human friendship that contained within itself the forgiveness of sin. When we think of the forgiveness of sin we do not think of an act of human friendship but of a legal act of God. This is because we do not know Christ. We do not know the wholeness in which men are brought together in God. We do not know the Church. We do not know the Eucharist.

The gospel portrays Christ as sitting down to table with sinners. It sees this homely affair as a profound theological mystery, as the ending of an old world. The table is God's, and men at this table hardly know themselves and yet know themselves and each other for the first time.

For over a hundred years, scholars of every religious belief and of no belief have been trying to understand the relationship between the highly *theological* description of Christ in the New Testament and the actual historical man who was a real man and not a piece of walking theology. They came to think that the original Jesus had got *buried* under all these theological descriptions as Son of God and saviour. But in our day the truth is excitingly dawning in scholarly circles. The truth is the unique *gesture* of Christ which provoked in the primitive Christian community the description of him as Son and saviour. In these terms they were expressing what he had done *to them*. And thus the patient and honest thinker has been led at last to the heart of Christ which is the heart of all time. The Eucharist is the solemn celebration of that heart in our midst, and our gathering into it. It will change us in proportion as we understand and act out in our lives that identity between friendliness and Godliness that is the gesture of Christ.

What about it?

There are things in the gospel that seem obvious, that in a way *are* obvious, but really are strangely shocking. Take this one: 'If any man will come after me, let him deny himself, take up his cross, and follow me.' Our Lord is recorded as saying this during his public ministry, before there was any question of crucifixion. What on earth, then, could people have made of it? To us who hear it now it seems obvious. In the first place, what is our religion but a following of Christ? And in the second place, we know that suffering and death are part of our life, so what could be more obvious than the idea that we should *accept* these? And so we come to think that all the text is saying is that we must accept all that comes to us, encouraged in this by him who most perfectly accepted suffering and death.

But our Lord does *not* say '*accept* the cross'. He says 'take it up'. Death, for him, is not something that happens to us on the way. It *is* the way. Suffering is not something we take in our stride, it *is* our stride. And this is very surprising.

Is it not also thoroughly morbid? And if we are honest, do not these words have for us a morbid ring, 'only not morbid, because it's our Lord'? Are we not repelled by a certain pursuit of suffering that we seem to find in much of the Christian tradition?

We have to understand in far greater depth the Teacher who, unlike *all* other teachers, pointed to his death as the way. Christ does not lay down axioms for the good life. He holds up life itself before our eyes, and life in its actual concrete totality, the life that advances to death. He represents it all, in himself. He *does* it at us. And he says, 'Well, what about it?' Supposing at a party someone suddenly cried out, 'Look, I'm going to die. What about it?' We should be thoroughly embarrassed. We'd be made conscious of ourselves and of our life as a mass of indecision and compromise. Well, that's what Christ is doing to us, but in a strangely authoritative way that no one can get round. Christ does not call for good resolutions. He calls for a *decision*. He, the completely decided man, thrusts himself on us half-living, half-undecided and fearful people, and says, 'What about it? Behold, I stand at the door and knock.'

The Sacred Heart

'One of the soldiers pierced his side with a spear, and at once there came out blood and water.' St John, the most initiated of the evangelists, sees a deep meaning in this event. And a very old tradition has seen in the piercing of Christ's side and the outflowing of blood and water, the birth of the Church. The new life pours forth *in answer* to the attack of man on Christ. There is a lot to think about here.

We must first ask: what was it about Jesus that provoked the crucifixion? Well of course it was his opposition to the established religious attitudes of which the authorities were the custodians. But more basically, it was the fact that he was so much more *alive* than other men: and men dread and fear a fulness of life in someone, and the fear turns to hatred. And so the crucifixion was the conflict between life and the fear of life, between human truth and the human lie. It had to be. Put Jesus and other men side by side, and you get the cross.

The next thing to notice is this. This death, which men inflicted on Jesus, was what his whole being asked for. For this fully alive man saw death as his consummation. The more alive, the more awake a man is, the more he sees death *right ahead*. Whereas we who are only half-alive, see it out of the corner of our eye. Christ saw death right ahead of him, as his fulfilment.

And so men, in crucifying our Lord, fulfilled him. Underlying this savage conflict, there was a sort of unity between his desire and theirs. Calvary is a tempestuous love affair between Christ and man.

This is the very stuff of life. Lovers in their act of love are within an ace of destroying each other. There is an instinct to break what is beautiful in order to get life from it. And make no mistake: the more you have in you, the more people will crucify you to get at it.

It is because of its closeness to the deepest things in life that Calvary can never grow old. And the closer we come to ourselves and to an appreciation of what we are and of what we do to each other, the more we know the blood that has renewed the world.

God's love in Christ comes forth *in answer to* sin, not *in spite of* sin. That is the lesson of the spear. I am not to say, 'I am a miserable sinner and yet Christ died for me.' No, Christ dies by my hand and so encloses me in the tide of his blood, his spirit, his new life. Christ did not die to make me feel small. He died to enlarge me.

Thus we clear up the muddle into which God and history settle down in the lazy Christian mind, and clear the stage for the daring leap of faith. Then we begin to understand how, on the cross, history, harbouring in a baffling coincidence the oppositions of sin and grace, shivers with the liberating mystery of God.

III

CHRIST AND FREEDOM

Christmas

EVERY CHRISTMAS I find myself wondering whether we have ever really understood Christ, understood this new life that has come among us. This is purely the way it should be. Christ, like someone we desperately love, should be a perpetual surprise, a continuous fresh start.

We visit the crib. We hear once again the conventional phrases about the Son of God appearing in the most humble circumstances. These sentiments can be very misleading, for they convey the idea of a visitor from a higher power coming to us in lowly attire—one of the stock themes of fairy tales. You know, the simple girl who is kind to this apparently unimportant and sometimes even repulsive stranger: then off goes the disguise, and the simple peasant girl finds herself married to a great prince. This is beautiful, but it is not the Christian message, the Christmas message. Christ is not a prince in disguise—*he is a man*.

And the lesson of the crib is that through the wonderful act of God, *man* is heir to the universe. Man is set free from a childish religion of walking in step with powers beyond his ken, like a child who walks along the pavement carefully avoiding the cracks between the paving-stones with which mysterious dangers are associated. Christ has given us a mature and manly relationship with God. We are sons, with the freedom of the house. God demands of us, not the petty little conformisms of pagan religion, not the minute observance of laws, but the free generous acts with which men go to meet life.

New life

The New Testament gives us two great descriptions of the new life, the Christian life: that of our Lord and that of St Paul.

For our Lord, the new life is human living as we know it, but intensified, realized in the present moment, and given to God—and the test of whether we *have* given it to God is whether we still worry about the future and the past. I get more and more from the gospels the impression that people, in comparison with Christ, are only half-alive. Christ is life itself, hammering on the tombs in which our souls lie buried.

For St Paul, this new life is a more mysterious and theological business. It involves plunging, through baptism, into death with Christ and rising in him to a new life, a new community, the Church, the Body of Christ. You know, St Paul actually thought the Christian had already died, was really dead. It was on this ground that he argued our freedom from the law, for the law obviously cannot touch the dead.

Both concepts, our Lord's and St Paul's, fit perfectly together. It is a difference of perspective only. Our Lord is *ahead* of us, beckoning us his way, the way of all-renunciation and joyful death. St Paul, as it were, describes this journey *from the side*. Paul alerts us to the *mystery* of Christ. Christ warns us that there is nothing vague or esoteric about the mystery.

Religious freedom

With the passing of the Council's decree on religious freedom, the Church throws away her crutches and walks anew in the confidence of the resurrection. She exorcizes the spectre of the Catholic state, in which the common man is ruled, whether he likes it or not, on Catholic principles. The City of God is not governed by a temporal monarch. It is ruled by faith, hope and love. This rule of faith is indeed given to us by the pope and the episcopal college, but only to those who in conscience and in faith accept it as giving expression to the unity they enjoy. I obey the pope because I am a Catholic. I am not a Catholic because I obey the pope.

Nothing, absolutely nothing, must impede the process whereby Christ our Lord freely calls free men and women into the fellowship of his risen life and sends them into a darkened world that is hungry for love and meaning. This and this alone. Christ and Christ alone. No longer must this joyful offer of Christ be obscured by ecclesiastical ifs and buts. We are learning to look people straight in the eyes.

Billy Graham

I find Billy Graham a most impressive person. But something strikes me very forcibly about his presentation of the faith. Once on television an atheist said to him, 'Do you attribute earthquakes to man's sin?'—and Graham answered, in effect, 'Yes'! He takes the story of paradise absolutely literally and, more than that, extends it to make it say *much* more than it does. Originally everything in the garden was lovely, and everything was garden. Man, planted by a loving creator in this cosmic garden, rebelled against God and gummed up the whole cosmic works, yes, unleashed all the destructive forces of nature.

Now first of all, this astounding assertion is not required by orthodox Christian faith. And a man who feels the need to frame his faith in this way is an example *not* of faith but *in a way* of the lack of it. Real faith thrives miraculously and divinely in the very thick of life's complexity, of the inbuilt doubt of mortal man. It does not have to cultivate a garden to grow in. It does not have to domesticate the universe in order to live in it. Sometimes on a building site you will see a dandelion that has forced its way up, God knows how, through layers of concrete. That's what real faith is like. It lives absolutely cheek-by-jowl with doubt, with the huge uncertainty that we feel in ourselves. And the most amazing thing of all is that in spite of this it makes, here and there, jolly good sense of the world. It does this because it makes sense of *you*, and this in spite of the periods of blackout where it makes no sense at all. Indeed these periods contribute to the strength of faith. Faith thrives on darkness, as a man's love for a woman will grow in the absence of those easier assurances from her which young love requires.

IV

CHRISTIANS AND OTHERS

Christian loss of nerve

WE HEAR much today of a loss of nerve on the part of Christians. The present Pope is sensitively aware of this. It happens, I think, as follows. Although the Church knows that her primary concern is with a human welfare that lies beyond the confines of this world, still a very important element in her self-confidence is a conviction that she can contribute significantly to man's temporal well-being. It would take too long to say why this is so, but it *is* so. The mediaeval Church that proclaimed with such force the message of eternal salvation was a Church that knew she had been largely responsible for the civilizing of Europe.

Today the Church looks out on a world that is building its own civilization. She knows she has had only a small hand in the human achievements of that civilization: the abolition of slavery; the attempted abolition of war; the war on want; the great social services. She looks aghast at her feeble reaction to the slaughter of five million Jews. And she begins to wonder: can it really be that I possess the whole meaning of human life if I make so little difference to this desperate world?

But that is only half the picture. There is, just round the corner, a colossal loss of nerve on the part of this new *world* that is coming into being. Our whole preoccupation is with *adjustment*: adjusting the so-called 'social misfit' to society. In all our concerns, whether over delinquency or Vietnam, there is the basic notion of a *norm* to which the present situation must be adjusted. Now the more people think this way, the more they are heading towards the point where they must ask: *what is this norm worth?* What are we supposed to *do* with the life that we have tidied up?

The Church is the only society that really cares about this question.

Cleansing the temple

The cleansing of the temple symbolizes the inauguration of perfect religion: the love of God taking complete possession of man, and expressing itself in man's love of his neighbour as himself.

We often hear it said today that a man can love his neighbour without 'bringing God in'. This is the standpoint of contemporary atheistic humanism. Certainly there is today much love of neighbour that does not acknowledge a religious basis. Some English religious sisters who recently visited charitable institutions in Sweden were amazed at how much people are prepared to do for each other nowadays without seeing any need to believe in God.

But the Christian demand is that I love my neighbour *as myself*. I certainly *approach* such love whenever I say to myself 'Why should I have money, health, freedom, status, education, and not he?'—and draw some practical conclusions. But I have not *attained* such love until I hold him my equal in *every respect*; until I attach the same value to *that man over there* as I do to *this man in here*, this immediately and warmly felt being that I am; until I spring to my neighbour's aid with the same urgency with which I react to a personal slight or withdraw my toe from a too-hot bath.

Now I simply have not got in myself the standpoint for thus seeing my neighbour as my equal. I am committed in the very nature of things to feeling more attached to myself than to my neighbour: for I *am* myself. The only standpoint from which I and my neighbour are really *equal* is *God's* standpoint. And so it is only in so far as I am lifted to God's standpoint that I can love my neighbour as myself. That this raising is possible, and that in fact it does happen through God's grace, is the substance of the Christian message.

All Souls

There is a profound difference between the Christian faith in immortality and the belief in an after life such as we find it in some pagans. In the pagan view, man is a soul imprisoned temporarily in a body. Death releases the soul from this captivity and enables it to take its place among the immortals. You will notice two things about this belief. First, death is itself the soul's release. Secondly, this is an individual adventure of the soul, having nothing whatever to do with our togetherness.

The Christian belief is profoundly different. First, death begins our immortal existence *not* because it releases the soul from the body, but because the death of the Christian is his full and final joining to the death of Christ, *in* whom he is to rise again. And to rise in Christ is to rise as a member of the Body of Christ. This brings us to the other big difference between pagan and Christian immortality. Christian immortality is *social*. Christ rose from the dead *a new man*, of whom we are members.

When we pray for the dead we remember that we too shall die. Let us see to it that we do both these things in a Christian and not a pagan way. That is to say, we should not think of our dead relations and friends as *on their own* but as members with us of Christ's triumphant body. We should, as it were, pray them more closely into the unity of that Body, extending to them the single indivisible love that binds us all together in Christ. And secondly, when we think of *our* death, we should not desire to be saved *apart*, but to be *a* part of that which is saved, the glorious Body of Christ, the Holy Church.

Let our holy communion be what holy communion always really *is*: a communion, in Christ, of the living and the dead. May Christ send his Spirit anew among us, so that we may grow into this vision, this communion of saints, this hope. For it is this alone, it is love alone, that is proof against the despair of this world. It is this alone that can give hope to the world. We Christians have a long way to go before we can radiate this hope. As long as we are preoccupied with our own salvation, we are hoarding the bread of which the world stands in need.

Veritatem facientes in caritate

What is happening to people today? Life is getting more and more complicated, the machine is moving faster and faster, requiring of us, its parts, that we become smoother and smoother. Human relations today are more and more modelled on the smooth running of a machine. The 'virtue' of today is not mutual candour but mutual evasion. We do not seek to reach our brother's heart; we aim not to get in his hair.

And meanwhile people's real selves are disappearing more and more into the hidden recesses of personality, where they are never shown even to their owner. We live in a profound solitude, creating a superficial social self to meet the demands of the machine. Symptomatic of all this is our obsessive concern with 'the image', the continuous succession of smooth phrases, the whole 'with-it' culture.

But the self, in living, builds up a massive discontent and frustration which bursts forth in new and unheard-of crimes, and in every form of mental and nervous disorder. And out of these depths of solitude people desperately seek communion in the flesh, which is so often a kind of intimacy without sincerity.

This picture is our version of original sin; the captivity from which Christ would set us free.

Paul's hymn to charity

If asked what is the most convincing account of itself that the Christian faith has ever given, I should reply without hesitation 'Paul's hymn to charity' (1 Corinthians 13). Anyone who really understands that hymn must be a believer. Charity according to St Paul pushes out beyond all moral attitudes, however excellent. First, it takes you to the point where no moral attitude seems possible, where continued forgiveness of others is against reason, where a man is exposed to this bitter world in all its naked irrational strength, and it says 'even here, nay especially here, love survives'. Secondly, it makes us *see* that charity, which pushes out beyond all moral attitudes, pushes out also beyond the confines of this life.

Here are some bitter words of André Malraux.

'You know what they say: "It takes nine months to create a man and only a single day to destroy him." It does *not* take nine months to make a man. It takes fifty years—fifty years of sacrifice, of determination, of—so many things! And when that man has been achieved, when there is no childishness left in him, nor any adolescence, when he is truly, utterly a man—the only thing he is good for is to die.'

He who has heard Paul's words with his innermost heart can

agree with this account—only he will agree with utter joy, whereas Malraux wrote in despair.

All Saints

People seem to think of God as a spectator on the touchline of life, noting the merits and the faults of the players with a view to rewarding them at the end of the game. In reality, God is the *goal*, on which all life, this whole vast universe, is converging. Our Lord said, 'I, if I be lifted up, will draw all things to myself.' And he permits us to catch a hint of this process in history—for is it not clear that the human race today is striving and stumbling towards unity? Unity. That is the watchword today: in the Church and in the world. God is found in unity, and unity is found in God. So when you forgive your enemy, or when you go out of your way to help your brother, you are to think of this, not as an isolated event for which God awards a mark, but as a step towards unity, towards God. With each such step, life makes more sense, and the more God is in it.

The theme of All Saints puts us in mind of those generous souls who have entered whole-heartedly and without hesitation into this grand process of God. They, gathered now into one in God, constitute the spearhead in that evolution whose goal *is* God.

The Church

'The gates of hell shall not prevail against it.' We have heard these words since we were children. This is one of the few

bible texts that have entered every Catholic classroom. It conjures up an image of a city under seige, the enemy battering
at the gates, to no avail. Wait a minute, though! Something's
gone wrong. We see the enemy battering at the *gates of the
Church*, but our Lord says it is the *gates of hell* that don't
prevail. We've got the whole thing wrong. It's the Church, not
the foe, that's on the offensive. The forces of evil are on the
defensive, trying to keep the Church *out*, not trying to break *in*.

What then is this force of evil that is on the defensive? It
is the deep inertia in the heart of man, not wanting to be
disturbed. It is the paralysing force of custom, of routine, of
what we're used to. It is the voice that says, 'I'm all right, leave
me alone.' Against the old, old citadel of man, the new power
of Christ's love is unleashed, and the old does not prevail.
Christ pressed home his attack, and the citadel was goaded
into the offensive. It rose against Christ and crucified him. And
out of the crucified body of Christ there flowed the new life
that overcomes all evil.

Now once we get the picture right, two things follow. First,
although we are that victorious Church of which Christ speaks,
the battle is in and among *ourselves*. We are not perfectly the
Church. In part—a very large part—we are the old man who
has still to surrender to Christ's love and become the Church.
Second, in so far as we have succumbed to the power of love,
we are committed to winning others to that power, to taking
an active part in that raid on the heart of man that the Church
is all about.

Many Catholics today are disturbed: the Church seems to be
losing her power, her prestige; they no longer have before them
the magnificent if vague image of a solid immovable rock with-
standing the waves. It is indeed disturbing. It is always disturbing to realize that a job we thought of as belonging to someone
else is really *our* job. It is always disturbing to realize that *I've*
got to do more.

Let's get one thing absolutely clear and never forget it. The
Church is the community of love and forgiveness, and propa-

gates itself by the exercise of those two God-implanted virtues. Let's face it, isn't it because we haven't got the thing down to these basic terms that our communions seem to make so little difference?

Christian rage

By far the most serious objection to the Christian Faith is the intolerance, the rigidity and the cruelty of Christians. From the moment that Christianity was accepted as the state religion in 325 A.D., Christians began persecuting non-believers and heretics and Jews. It is an appalling history. In the sphere of morals, too, the Christian image has been one of condemnation and ostracism rather than of love. If I were an unbeliever trying to find my way to faith, I should find this by far the hardest nut to crack.

And yet, if we face this problem head-on, and do not engage in the hopeless task of explaining away the vast back-log of Christian and Catholic intolerance, a surprising thing happens: we get a precious new insight into the truth. Let me explain.

Just think what it means for poor, weak, immature man to be entrusted with the very truth of God. Is it surprising that it should take at least a couple of thousand years for him to grow up humanly to this new status conferred on him by God? Of course he will not be fully grown up to it until the end of time, but this means he does grow towards it *with* time and *in* time. Christian man in the past has been like someone raised suddenly from the anonymity of the ranks to V.I.P. status. He has shown all the marks of the jumped-up officer: the insecurity, the jealousy of his new-found status, the pomposity, the insistence that he is in the right, not daring to give an inch.

Now is the time for heart-searching, and this is a probing

B

deeper into the heart of the Christian thing, the humility of the cross, the serene confidence of the resurrection.

Archbishop Ramsey in Rome

When the Archbishop of Canterbury visited Rome, the Pope talked of 'the Church of Rome and the Church of Canterbury', and of building a bridge between them. This was hardly what we were brought up to! If anyone had used the language five years ago he'd have been sharply corrected.

What then is happening? The whole world is becoming newly self-conscious, and in the midst of the development Christians are seeking to understand anew in simplicity and depth what is the Christian commitment. I think that the Christians of the future will be known, not by a mass of dogmas, but by a simple, humble, joyous, full-of-hope YES to life. This is not to say that the dogmas will be bypassed. No, they will be better understood, centred in the simplicity of the Christ-awakened heart, and of course, as we come to understand them in this way and not as fixed things in their own right, we find ourselves quite differently related to those other Christians, represented by the Archbishop of Canterbury, who have grown up with a different slant on the Christian dogmas. The pace of unity quickens as the Christian heart quickens. Catholics and Anglicans at this time look joyfully to their two leaders who have had the courage to give official expression to this quickening Christian pace. After years of Christian caution, we are beginning to see at work the impatience of the Spirit.

The Pope at UNO

The Pope told the UN that we must all learn to think of man in a new way. Five years ago, Pope John told the Council: 'We are on the eve of a new order in human relations, which in the due providence of God will be brought to completion.'

This is the voice of the Spirit in our time. It bears the mark of the Spirit, for it is *original* in both senses: in the sense of 'new' and in the sense of 'going back to the origins'.

How we restrict the influence of God in the world! What a narrow, provincial view we have of this influence! We confine it to the visible Church, and we equate God's fortunes with its fortunes. Meanwhile, in the wide world where the human *agon* is working itself out, God is teaching us all sorts of things that our narrow minds are reluctant to grasp. The substance of the Christian fact is the brotherhood of man. But man comes into this brotherhood only through a radical recreation of himself in his personal, social, sexual, mortal being. To a world in search of this brotherhood, the Church represents this deep and mysterious dimension of brotherhood. And this means that the Church must take with full seriousness all those things in the modern world that express the yearning for brotherhood. She has to see in the United Nations, not the purely political attempts of man to find a political solution, but the matter of a sacrament, to be penetrated and consecrated, rather as in the past she consecrated kingship. Of this consecration, the visit of the Pope to the United Nations is a *symbol*. Whether it is a strong and efficacious symbol, or whether it is an empty symbol, depends on the effort of the entire Church, of all of us, to enter into the heart of the world of today. The Church must listen, intently and humbly, to the world: and in the act of loving attention she will become frankly conscious of the life that is in her; a life that is not of this world, but *for* this world. The old formula was '*in* the world, not *of* the world'. We must do better than this: 'not *of* the world, but *for* the world.'

V

NOW

Advent

IN ADVENT, we, the community of God, attune ourselves to God's coming. God's coming is every moment. God is he who comes.

We have lost the full meaning of these words. We see God's coming as a thing of the past and a thing of the future, not as a thing of NOW. We think of this present time as a sort of interim period between the first coming and the second. But an interim government is put in by people who don't know what they want. That's the trouble with us Christians: we have forgotten who we are and what we are about. We look *back* on the events of Christ's life. We look at the events of today with a sort of Christian bewilderment. We puzzle over Christ's discourse about the end of the world—why, we wonder, does he say that this catastrophic event is 'even now at your doors'? And we look in a detached way at the distant tableau of the second coming. We have lost our bearings.

The remedy is to believe with passionate conviction that God is a present happening in the Church in the world. This means that with every true prayer, and with every work done in his grace, and especially with every strengthening, by such work as the bond between us, God comes, God acts in the world. In every moment the Church, the community of God, comes into being. This is Advent. We only meditate on his coming at Bethlehem and at the end to increase our conviction of his coming now, in our work, our prayer, our love, our common life, our liturgy.

Epiphany

Why do we go to Mass on Epiphany? What little most of us know about the feast makes us wonder still more. What on earth is so important about those kings and camels?

But in fact this 'little Christmas', as the Irish call it, ranks in the Church's estimation above Christmas itself. In it we celebrate Christ's *manifestation* to us. The story of the Magi is just a convenient peg on which to hang this massive idea.

How does the manifestation of Christ to us come to rank above his being *born* into this world? Because the centre of the Christian faith is not a bare historical fact, but an actual meet-up between the living God and you and me. As with a great love, we enjoy thinking about the beloved before we met him, when he was going through all the tiresome business of going to school etc., but the moment we love to dwell on is the moment when we did meet him, a moment which continues up to the present time. And so the Church feels closer to Christ as she here and now bathes in his light than when she thinks of him in the past. On the Epiphany she hears the words of the prophet: 'Arise and shine, Jerusalem, for thy light is come, and the glory of the Lord is risen upon thee.'

The real presence

There is a disturbing feeling in the air today that the old Catholic certainties are going. Even the real presence of Christ in the Eucharist seems to be undergoing revision. The new emphasis on the Eucharist as a community meal seems to take the spotlight off the sacred host, whose holiness used to convince us, irrespective of the community.

I am convinced—and I make bold to say that this conviction, now growing in the Church, is of the Holy Spirit—that this new way of thinking, far from taking away the traditional certainties, is allowing them to speak to us with their original force. Christ is far more eloquently present in the Eucharist if his presence is seen as the luminous centre of a community itself filled with new light and life. Far more powerfully so than if I think of the presence as an isolated miracle.

Incidentally, the Second Vatican Council came so far in this direction that its Constitution on the Liturgy has this to say: 'Christ is present not only in the priest and assembly, but also in the sacred elements themselves.' You see what has happened? We've got past the stage of putting it the other way round, that 'Christ is present not only in the sacred elements but in the community as well'. The Church now sees Christ as firmly in its midst, as the bedrock reality, and it is in this context that she sets her understanding of the Eucharist.

Here is a comparison for understanding the change that is going on. Imagine for a moment a world permanently in darkness. In the dark sky there reigns a beautiful, solitary star. That star is the wonder of the dark world. Poets sing its praises. Then, by some impossible astronomical shift, the earth comes into orbit of this star, which becomes *the sun. Now* the beauty of that star is known in a million ways, in deep blue oceans, in the waving of corn, sheep and cattle, in the faces of men. *But* the old poetry has gone ... yet what sane man could regret its passing?

Private prayer and public liturgy

It is frequently said nowadays that the new emphasis on public liturgical worship is squeezing out the idea of private prayer. It is observed that people do not remain in church after Mass the way they used to. One hears stories—never to be trusted—of German and Dutch priests positively discouraging private prayer. One also hears it said that there has been too big a swing from the love of God to the love of our neighbour as the main influence in religion. And Malcolm Muggeridge has made a scathing and amusing comment on 'the Catholic Church getting with it'. At last, he says, she has grown tired of the thankless task of persuading men to look beyond this world and prepare for death, and she has chosen instead to offer herself to the world as a kind of oil for the social works: madly agreeing with what everyone is doing, and saying 'we'll help you do it even better'. We hear a good deal about alleged loss of nerve on the part of Christians.

There is some truth in these observations. There *is* a swing taking place from the 'Garden of the Soul' to the wild, wide world of today. But we lose sight of something vitally important when we think in these terms, when we think of personal religious experience and communal life as *alternatives*. We are forgetting something important—and what an understatement that is! For what we are forgetting is GOD. God is altogether beyond this opposition between personal and social. In prayer, in *live* prayer, man is, all at once, supremely himself and supremely 'for the others'. That is the very meaning of God (may he, who alone can do it, make this clear to us. May he show us his face and, in so doing, give us faces to know each other by.) I think that a Christian who has begun to understand this meaning will cease to think of God and his neighbour as two separate claimants on his attention and love. For him, the problem of reconciling the love of God and the love of neighbour will be seen to be a false problem, posed in terms of a God who has never existed and a neighbour seen with the dull eye of custom.

Someone said to me the other day—she was a devoted Catholic—'The Church seems to have so little to do with God.' That is the crux of the matter. And the obverse of it is that God seems to have little to do with the Church, little to do with this association of men and women.

If the Church today seems to be losing itself in this world, it is really to rediscover herself in Christ, who identified himself with this world to the point of death and transforms it in his resurrection. It is in the resurrection and the new community that it creates, that the living God is found.

VI

GOD

I ONCE HELD A TEACH-IN with atheists. One said to me: 'If an earthly father neglected his children as the heavenly father does, he'd be sent to prison.' The speaker was a Jew, most of whose family had disappeared into the maw of Nazi Germany.

I wonder if any of us can really answer this charge against God out of the depths of our being and not merely by saying, 'That's a wicked, blasphemous way to talk.'

The man who really believes in God is not the man whom God has protected from the shocks of life. It is the man who, abandoned by God, has not surrendered to our inbuilt bitterness, has not allowed his heart to go dead, has continued to say 'yes' to life. Deep within ourselves are the two choices: to go positive, or to go negative. The real God is the God we acknowledge, whether knowingly or not, when we go positive. He withdraws his *external* support in order that we may discover him *within ourselves*, for thus only do we discover him as he really is.

Now in this desperate choice, for life or for death, for being positive people or negative people, we depend *on each other*. It is the smile of recognition and the helping hand that opens the closed heart to God. And thus the only answer to the atheist is to love him. It is a terrible thing to leave him alone and unloved and tell him he ought to believe in God. In so doing we force upon him a God who does not exist, a God who is not the God of love. Of this crime so many Christians have been guilty. All Christians who persecute in the name of Christ are guilty of it.

God today—I

If you find the idea of God uninteresting, there's something terribly wrong with your idea of God. But it would be dishonest to leave the matter there, to say 'If you don't find God exciting, then it's your fault.' We have to ask the far more radical question: *is* the idea of God interesting as it comes over to us in sermons, prayer books, pronouncements of Church authorities? Is it not true to say that all the hallowed phrases in which God is described are phrases coined long ago and now repeated by the Church almost in her sleep.

I am sure that if I were not a Christian I should say: 'Yes, I suppose there's a God, but I wonder what that means to me. The Church, which is supposed to tell me what it means, is obviously living in the past, repeating a lesson learned long ago.'

Why has the idea of God gone dead on us? Because *we* are dead, and have lost the art of looking to God to quicken us. We are dead to each other, and so God is dead to us. Our Lord warned us of this. He said his Father was all love, all forgiveness. But he said: 'If you don't forgive your brother from the heart, then God—yes, this God who is nothing but love—will not forgive you.' That is to say, he will not *be* God, he will not *be* love, to you. He who ignores his brother switches God off, as it were. If we are content that the world around us be desert, then we do not want the rain. We do not even know what the rain is: the Holy Spirit of God.

It is this human desert that we have lived in and become accustomed to, that has made the idea of God remote, old, and dead. The idea of God will live again when our prayer makes us conscious of how unprofitable we are to other people, and when the pronouncements of the Church are full of sorrow at the vast human failure for which she is always responsible. The soul of man is like a tree. It stretches up ecstatically to the light, but it does so out of roots that go deep and wide into the soil. Our roots are gone dead, or else they feel around them not the rich soil of charity, but the stones of indifference, and so our prayer is languid, our idea of God pale and conventional.

At this time the Church is waiting to speak newly of God out of the depths of human experience and commitment to the needs of men today. She waits to speak again *prophetically*, to bring up through the rubble of centuries the prophecy that is in her, as Pope Paul said in his opening address to the final session of Vatican II.

'I will take the heart of stone out of the midst of you,' says God in the prophecy of Ezekiel, 'and put in you a heart of flesh.' A Catholic poet of the last century said 'Thou, O thou, Lord of life, send my roots rain.' The quickening of the roots is the rebirth of love among ourselves. In this quickening to our neighbour, God is known once again as the living God. There is no other way, and this is a sure way. On every page of the New Testament you will find two things: the majesty of God and the love of the brethren. These are the two sides of the one coin: the hard currency of the Spirit.

God today—II

We are very busy. And when one is very busy, the most important things get forgotten. The Church is busy. And so she forgets God. The Bishop of Woolwich was busy—until one day he slipped a disc and was laid up. Then he started thinking about God. The first thing he realized was that all the images with which we think of God, all the language in which we talk

of him, nearly all the language in which we pray to him, belong
to an age which is dead and gone. What a way to treat God!
Suppose a man were to treat his wife that way. Suppose that
after twenty years of married life he were to talk to her as the
sweet little thing he met at that never-to-be-forgotten party!

In every age, man feels his poverty in a way peculiar to that
age. Out of *that* experience of poverty, out of *those* depths, he
gropes after the strong comfort of God. He comes to see God
as the remedy for his particular ills. For ancient man, this
poverty consisted in an inability to cope with plague and all the
other visitations of nature, an inability to think for himself
politically, and a desire for ceremonial and colour. And so his
God was he who alone could give comfort in temporal affliction,
he who ruled over the city and was decked out in the splendour
of monarchy.

Today, the nature of man's poverty has dramatically and
rapidly changed. What you might call the human *centre of
gravity*, the human sense of the weight of the human condition, has shifted. Our poverty is the growing sense of *meaninglessness* in a world that we have tied up to an extent that
mediaeval man could not have dreamed of. If he *had* dreamed
of it, he would have thought the dream a blasphemy. Our
poverty is the frightful shallowness that creeps into personal
relationships in a technological age. The big thing *we* have to
learn about God is this: that when I don't love him, my
brother appears as something less than human. Find your
brother, really find him and cherish him regardless of creed,
class and colour, and God is in your midst. Not as a vague,
deeper dimension of human existence—this is where the Bishop
of Woolwich missed out—but as the Person who graciously and
freely gives the meaning and rains down the soft dew of the
Spirit.

The total ascent to God—I

The most basic thing in this universe is movement. Everything is on the move. *Nothing* is still. As far as we are concerned, 'to be' and 'to be on the move' are the same thing.

The simplest kind of movement is what we call local motion: the movement of a thing from one place to another. Have you ever thought about this? Probably not, for there's not an awful lot to think about here. The genius of Newton discovered *how* bodies move, what laws they obey. He didn't ask what movement really means, and the question doesn't make much sense.

But from this simple base, the universe works up to more and more complex and interesting kinds of movement. The movement of the plant pushing its way up through the soil is not a movement from place to place. It is that extraordinary thing called growth. Then we come to animals. The movement of a lion towards its prey bears only a superficial resemblance to the movement of a football. Basically, it is that extraordinary *restlessness* that we call life. Finally there is the restlessness of the human mind. The movement of the mind, too, is a movement of material things *and* a movement of life *and* something more. It is YOU. In you this whole restless universe comes to a head. It tosses and turns like a man that cannot sleep. Man is the insomnia, the fever of the universe. In him, the restlessness of the universe becomes a *questioning*.

To his questioning, man *cannot* find the answer in this world: for the simple reason that every movement in this world is only a poor version of the movement of man's mind. It is man that gives meaning to the swirling world. *But what is the meaning of man?* And whether we like it or not, and however clever we may be at evading it, this is the God-question. The whole universe converges on man, and in him cries out to God.

The universe is a convergence of one-way streets with man at the centre. He cannot go down any of the streets in search of rest, for all the traffic of the universe is *towards* him. There is no way back, and man's *only real future* is God.

The total ascent to God—II

Over a hundred years ago, Charles Darwin published his great work *The Origin of Species*. It caused consternation in religious circles. It has taken just a hundred years to discover that Darwin's central insight provides the key to a new approach to God: an approach far more exciting and all-embracing than was possible in the ancient world.

Darwin's central insight was this. He saw the basic *similarity* between different species of animal, as many others had, but he saw it in a new way. This similarity became to him a most eloquent fact. It was as if nature spoke to him and said 'Can't you see how basically simple I am? In the vast tracts of time at my disposal, I progressively *elaborate* the patterns that you have observed. I evolve the jellyfish into man.'

A hundred years later, a new genius was to extend Darwin's insight. He was the Jesuit, Pierre Teilhard de Chardin. He saw the evolutionary sweep as extending from the very simplest material to the most complex. And thus he saw the whole universe as revving up to the white heat of conscious being, that is man (and of course any other conscious beings there may be in the universe). And this sparks off the God-question: if man is the meaning of the universe, what is the meaning of man?

The most fascinating thing about this approach is that it

unites the *two* approaches to God so far produced by the Christian tradition. For St Thomas argued to God from the universe, while St Augustine argued from the restlessness of the human heart. Now we understand that the restlessness of man *is* the movement of the whole universe seeking its meaning.

Pentecost

If there is any idea more than another that is coming to dominate our age and explain us to ourselves, that is the idea of *relation*. We understand, as never before, that everything in our lives is relative. If we are wise, we are learning to approach our difficulties with people in a new way: no longer saying how *wrong* they are and how *right* we are, but trying to *understand* the relationship between our two personalities, what we are doing to each other. Social workers approach their task not in a moral and condemnatory spirit but in an effort to understand, and to form creative relationships.

Now we Christians believe, or say we believe, in God. More than that, we claim to meet God in our lives. But God is *not* relative. He is the absolute truth. And yet we know—especially today we know—that we never meet absolute truth in our lives. In our dealings with people, all is relative.

How do we put the two together? We can only do so if we think of God as an all-embracing and all-penetrating wholeness. He cannot occupy a *corner* in our lives. His coming to us must be the transforming of all our experience of ourselves and of each other. Gone for good—and gone for *our* good—is the notion of a God whom we could even be tempted to think of as one *among* the factors of life.

That is the meaning of Pentecost, when God finalizes his coming to us in the Spirit poured out on all flesh.

God loves us

Have we ever really believed that God loves us? I'm sure
we haven't, although we were told so from our earliest years.
There was something wrong with the way we were told. Or the
people who told us didn't really believe it themselves. Let me
give some examples.

I remember, as a boy, a priest who gave us a retreat and
spoke in glowing terms about God's love. But when I went to
him with a moral problem, being uncertain as to whether I
had committed a sin, his advice was, 'Better confess it, just to be
on the safe side.' But good heavens, there's no 'safe side' of
someone who loves you, or rather there's no unsafe side. You
see, he preached the love of God, but in practise he treated
God as someone of whom one can't be too sure.

And then there was the way we were taught about sorrow
for sin. Of course we had to be taught this, but the *way* it was
taught tended, subtly, to play down the love of God. God
loved us, yes, but still we had to mind our 'p's and 'q's. We
were not told that to be sorry for sin is simply to allow God to
love us again— for no true lover imposes himself if he is not
wanted.

Then we were told that 'presumption' was a terrible sin, and
this certainly didn't help. God loves you, but don't take liberties.
The truth is that presumption is not an over-estimation of
God's love, but an under-estimation of it: treating God as
though he were indifferent to our response and would treat us
the same way whatever our feelings in the matter.

And then confession: God saying, 'Get your dirty soul clean
before you approach my nice clean table.' And that's all wrong.
Confession is a wonderful gift of God's love. It is an assurance
of his forgiveness, his forgiveness made *audible*.

And last, and by far the worst, hell. The darkest mystery of our religion. Here is the most difficult thing to understand *without* diminishing our sense of the love of God. But even hell is tied up with God's love. It is God's refusal to force himself on the unwilling. And remember this. When you are praying and trying to do God's will, and when you are sorry for not doing it—when in fact you are in *any* relation with God—*hell is out of the question*. It's right out of the picture. You are not walking on a tight-rope with hell below you. You are walking along a good solid road, and hell is a side-track you don't have to bother with.

What was wrong with our schooling was that there seemed to be so many 'buts' to God's love. God loves you *but* you mustn't presume. God loves you *but* you must not sin. God loves you *but* you must get your sin washed away. What we have to do is to change 'but' into 'therefore'. There are absolutely no 'buts' to God's love, no strings, no cautions. All the things in our religion that seemed to be qualifications of God's love are really so many rays of it, so many colours it takes.

I remember as a boy once reading a preparation for confession in a prayer book. It said: 'A wasp stings you: you crush it. And yet God, despite all your offences, has spared you.' How on earth could anyone who believed in God's love write that kind of stuff? It's as though what the man had in his mind was this: we don't see many signs of God loving us, so let's take the line that it's really very good of him even to let us live!

Indeed we don't see many signs of God's love. The reason is that our eyes are tight shut. The way to open them is this. Think of someone who loves you, and ask yourself, 'Why should he love me?' I should be surprised if you answered 'Because I'm really rather a nice person.' You'll get a hint of the great, free, undeserved love, of which all *our* loving is a reflection. But better still, make a new effort to love your neighbour. Anyone who really, with effort, cares for his neighbour, will come to appreciate—slowly—the love that encloses us all.

God alone

In prayer we are concerned with God alone. But this means that we are concerned only with God's will. For 'God' and 'God's will' are one and the same thing. And so when we pray we are concerned with the whole world to which we belong, in which we belong, in which that will is manifested and carried out.

That man is concerned with God alone who, in prayer, resolves with God's grace to forgive his enemy or to fulfil as perfectly as possible the day's tasks. *He* is *not* concerned with God alone who, when he comes to prayer, puts his enemy right out of his mind as a distraction, an irrelevance, an annoyance, and foresees the next day's work only as a necessity.

You see the paradox here? If we attend only to the ordinary meaning of words, we should have thought that it was the *second* man who was going for God alone, for he has shut out everything else; and that it was the *first* man who was *not* concerned with God alone, since he admits the whole world into his heart when he prays. But in fact it is the other way round.

If you come to understand this *in practice*: if you can come to know from experience what is the *real* difference between pure prayer and not-so-pure prayer, then you are well on the way. For you have the most precious insight that a Christian *can* have: into the generosity of God which takes into the sweep of his simple essence the world in which we live and grow towards him.

There are privileged moments when all this becomes unusually clear: when we *know* that the whole-hearted decision to forgive and accept someone introduces us into the simple depths of God.

VII

SIN AND FORGIVENESS

Christian forgiveness

WHAT IS A SINNER? Is it just 'someone who commits sins or who has committed a sin'? I don't think so, and neither does the New Testament. Christ is far more concerned with the effect that sin has on a man than with the thing he did. What effect does sin have on us? Well, it creates a habit, and so you could say that a sinner is a man with a bad habit or habits. But even this is not what the New Testament means by a sinner.

There is a still deeper effect of sin. It makes a man despair of himself. It shuts him up in a false humility that will not venture forth joyously into life. It says inside his head, 'I'm no good. Nobody wants me. I'm a write-off.' Have you ever noticed how, when you've had a row with somebody and said more than you should, you are cagey with that person? It's as difficult to be friendly with someone you've offended as it is to be friendly with someone who has offended you. Well, it is this cagey, shut-up, paralysed condition that the New Testament really means by the state of sin. It is a state of being closed against life. That is why it is called an offence against God, for God *is* life, God *is* the future, God *is* the broad uplands, God is the life that awaits you.

St Paul said that the law made sin worse. For when he had sinned, the law said, '*Now* you have had it. *Now* you've got God against you', and this shuts a man up in his sinfulness.

Christ came to forgive sin. Try and forget the usual meaning we give to this statement. Try to see what it really means in the light of what I have just said. To forgive sin is to give the sinner hope. It is to make it possible for him to thaw out. It is to say to him: 'Life awaits you again, you are accepted, you don't have to do the "unworthy" act, you are wanted, there's something you can do that no one else can do.'

Christ could not have forgiven sin if he had not been God. But equally, he could not have forgiven sin if he had not been a man. By his warm human approach to people, he persuaded them out of their self-constructed cages and made them become full human beings.

How can we think of God's forgiveness as a mere keeping the slate clean, when even man's forgiveness is better than that? For we do not reckon that a man has forgiven his brother if he merely says, stiffly, 'All right, we'll say no more about it'. We expect him to offer his hand. Is God *less* generous than man?

God has forgiven sins through Christ: that is to say, through the contact of a warm and abundant humanity. Christ gave sinners back their humanity, their dignity.

God continues to forgive sin through men: and not only through priests, but every time men forgive one another. Is it not terribly clear that when we refuse to forgive our brother we keep him in his sin, make it nearly impossible for him to open himself to the love and forgiveness of God? That is why Christ lays such tremendous stress on forgiving one another. 'Forgive us our trespasses as we forgive them their trespass against us.' Give us the new life, the new hope, that we can pass on, in our small measure, to our brother.

It is a sorry spectacle to see Christians who regularly kneel for the Lord's forgiveness in the confessional, adopting a hard and condemnatory attitude to the sin of others. Why is it so often the regulars at confession who are worst in this respect? Why are they often the worst advertisement for the forgiveness of sin: the people least likely to draw their brothers into the warmth of God's embrace?

God is love. He loves us, and he loves through us. If we do not try to realize this and put it into practice, then all our Catholic practice is in vain.

Sin

God loves us: and we sin. How do we put those two facts
together? What is the *picture* that emerges? Surely it is a
picture of God's love as something sad, regretful. Above all,
as something of no practical consequence. God's love, I think,
is not for *me* as I know and feel myself, but for something in me
that I don't have any experience of, something impossibly good
he would *like* me to be but which of course I never shall be.

Now this is as disastrously wrong as it could be. The cause of
the trouble is that word 'sinner'. By our constant use of it we
identify ourselves with our sin. Not only do I sin: I *am* a sinner,
I *am* sinful. Notice by the way that we don't normally do this
in our human relations. If I deceive someone to save me or him
embarrassment and he finds out, I don't say, 'O I'm just a liar,
that's all.' I say 'I'm terribly sorry, I just couldn't face it.' But
when dealing with God we think it proper to jumble ourselves
and our sin together. We downgrade *ourselves*. We make ourselves worth nothing. And somehow God loves this worthless
thing that I am. Isn't it good of him?

So we altogether miss the simple force of the statement that
God loves us, which is that God finds each of us a fascinating
and exciting person. And God's taste is excellent. Whatever
other people may think of us, God thinks a lot of us, and he's
right. *Sin* consists in disagreeing with God's estimate: in saying
'No, I'm really nothing to write home about.' Sin is the failure
to love ourselves as God loves us. Sin is the failure to accept
ourselves. Sin is that self-bullying that makes nonsense of the
beauty of creation and knocks the life out of everything. That's
why there is so little charity in our lives: our religion has locked
us up in a sterile penitence.

We've got to put our thinking about sin completely into re-

verse, and recover the enormous, unqualified encouragement
of God. And once we've got it in ourselves, once we've got ourselves right—and I don't mean once we have stopped sinning
—then we can pass on this encouragement. To make someone
feel he is worth something after all is the most wonderful thing
you can do for him. It can work miracles. It is the miracle of
God's love, bringing water out of stony places that have forgotten even the smell of water.

Sin again

Our sense of sin is much too private. We think of our sins
as something we could only talk to the priest about, in the darkness of the confessional. This means that we've got the wrong
idea as to what our sins are. For our real sin is not something
we don't want other people to know about. Look, I could tell you
what are the things in my life that make me fear the judgment
of God: and neither you nor I would be embarrassed. On the
contrary you would recognize yourself in what I said. What
I would be giving is a self-portrait which every Christian man
would recognize as his own. So here goes.

I am afraid of life and the demands it makes on me. I am
afraid of the love that is demanded of me. I am afraid of the
unknown, out of which might come at any time a demand I
could not meet. I am afraid of myself, alive to this world, no
way back. And in this fear I constantly duck my responsibilities. I turn away from the head-on confrontation with life and
people and their needs. I try to escape the situation of being a
man set by God in this world to suffer and to seek and to grow.
This is my sin. And it is yours. We try to undo what God has
done in making us. We flee the burden of being human. We
seek to be cosy, to be left alone. This is what sin is. And it is not

something to be ashamed of. It is something the Christian has learned to sorrow for. And our sorrow is shared. It is a common experience. It goes into the 'I confess' with which we precede our eucharistic celebration. No celebration without sorrow. And no sorrow without celebration in which we know the joy of God's forgiveness.

There *are* things in my life which it would embarrass me and you to tell you about. I mean the particular ways in which I, with my character and upbringing and prejudices, escape God. I mean the particular bolt-holes down which I run from the face and the love of God. But the essence of my sin does not lie in where I escape to, it lies in where I escape from. The essence of my sin does not lie in what Francis Thompson calls 'the labyrinthine ways of my own mind'. The essence of my sin lies bare before you. And it is yours.

The Christian is a man who grows out of the private sense of guilt into the mature and spiritual sense of sin. And in so doing he meets his brothers. If we had a real sense of sin we would be a force in society, meeting the demands of God whose intention, we know in Christ, is the renewal of society. It is time we woke up and moved to God, instead of keeping ourselves to ourselves, keeping our private appointment with guilt.

Sin yet again

'I was late for Mass. I didn't say my night prayers. I was disobedient. I didn't behave with my boy-friend. . . .' STOP! What are you confessing? How are you thinking of all that lot? Under what *heading* do they all fall? You are confessing *bad behaviour*. That's how you are thinking of sin: a sort of misbehaviour in God's nursery.

This isn't really an adult concept of sin at all. When we were children, goodness meant good behaviour. The adults around us did not expect us to *relate* to them and to realize our obligations in that person-to-person relationship. Obviously we weren't capable of this. So they laid down a pattern of behaviour: what good little boys and girls do. Then we grew older, and became conscious of our relationships to the adults. Gradually they changed in our eyes. They were *persons*, and we saw them as persons because we were becoming persons.

Now our relationship to God should grow in the same way. But it doesn't do so in the easy, obvious way in which our human relationships develop. If, at the age of nineteen, I say 'Sorry Mum', in a baby-voice, my mother turns to me as a woman and says, 'Don't be silly.' *But God can't do this*, because we can't see him. And so we grow up in relation to others and stay babyish in relation to God. We mend our quarrels as men and women, but we mend our quarrel with God in a baby-voice through the priest in the confessional. In our human relations, a pattern of *behaviour* gives way to a relation of person-to-person commitment and obligation; but in our affair with God, the pattern of behaviour persists unchanged.

Roman Catholic Oedipus

'I ate meat on Friday—I forgot it was Friday. No, I suppose that wasn't a sin but I feel happier if I mention it.' Why do people 'feel happier if they mention it'? Because in the Catholic soul there lurks a remnant of paganism. The essence of paganism is that the gods do not distinguish between things done on purpose and things done in ignorance. Not knowing the true God, the pagans identified the gods with those cruelly indifferent forces of nature that punish alike the sinful and the merely mistaken. The whole point of the tragedy of King

Oedipus was that he incurred the wrath of heaven by a shameful deed done in ignorance of the circumstances.

What is rather curious is that people do not seem to see anything *wrong* in 'liking to mention it'. For this means that they can see nothing wrong in having a concept of God that is blasphemous—blasphemous because it lines him up with the stupid, vengeful, spiteful, undiscerning gods of paganism.

This is the fault of our upbringing. The emphasis in our schooling was on God's rule rather than on God; on the sacraments rather than on the God we meet with *in* the sacraments. And so it comes as a surprise to us to learn that 'having a right estimate of God' is of the very essence of religion. We *must* correct this. How can we really pray to the living God if we behave in confession as though a mistake about the day of the week could come between us? Of course we don't really think this way—we don't really think at all, that's the trouble. If we used our reason in life as little as we use it in religion, we'd be starving in twenty-four hours.

The sins of the world

What an extraordinary thing language is, especially religious language. It can conjure up one set of images if you are thinking in one way, and a quite different set of images if you are thinking in some other way. A religious statement can come to have a quite different feel when someone gives us a new slant on it. Take for instance what we say every day at the Mass: 'Lamb of God, who takest away the sins of the world.' Now the effect of this statement entirely depends on what that word 'sin' conjures up for us. Unfortunately sin was probably the first religious word we learnt. It meant *you* being horrid. And so we learned that Christ had taken on and taken away all the horrid things we do and think. And so the phrase 'who takest away the sins of the world' makes us feel guilty. Somehow we were responsible for the sufferings of Christ. That's the picture, isn't it? It's not a *joyful* picture.

But think of sin quite differently. Think of it as the *ugliness* in life. Think of it as the *situation* in which people's ideals are shattered on the wall of hard fact. Think of it as the old people saying to the young, 'You'll get over it. You won't mind when you're my age.' Think of it as the drabness of life, as the deadening of the spirit by routine. Think of it as the *oldness*, the deadness, the numbness, the fear of stepping out of line.

It's *all this* that comes dramatically to an end on the cross. See death, and all is old and sad; see God in death, and all is suddenly new.

Examen

Gladstone once referred to 'people whose religion spoils their morality'. I want to indicate another danger, closely connected with what Gladstone was referring to: the danger of a person's religious life slowly *diverging* from the will of God as this is made known to him in daily life.

It is quite possible, for instance, that, day by day, a person may be contracting out of his real moral responsibilities, and at the same time regularly examining his conscience before confession in a way that does not 'pick up' the serious and growing moral flaw. It is possible that a person is allowing his marriage to deteriorate, by taking the line of least resistance, by being unimaginative, by not striving to allay a growing mutual mistrust; and to be examining his moral life by a set of trivial and perfunctory questions learnt at school—have I missed my morning and night prayers? Have I been uncharitable? (which is much too vague).

What we require is a personal questionnaire which, like a magnet, picks up the real and serious defects in our life. Remember that God's will is declared to us not so much in a set of general rules, as in *our actual situation*, the actual pattern of personal relationships—to wife, to growing children, to business colleagues, to friends—in which God's providence has set us. This questionnaire must be personal. We can't get it from a book. One way of drawing it up would be to examine, in some detail, one specimen day in our lives, with the question: 'Am I building up my relationships or just letting them slip?' Then, for my regular examination, I can watch out for *my typical* acts of commission and omission. In this way I expose my real moral existence to God's healing grace—as opposed to a kind of standard Catholic soul.

VIII

SEX

Sex and marriage

ON THIS MATTER of sex, the big divide between Church and modern society is this: that the Church believes in free love and modern society does not. This statement is not a gimmick, nor a risky paradox, nor a daring eye-catcher, but an exact statement of the truth.

For what is free love? It is *secure* love. I can only have genuine free love when I feel able to give myself totally to another person, knowing that the gift is accepted in the way I meant it. It is to break beyond the anguishing doubt as to whether we both mean the same thing by this act of love. A love for which this doubt remains *cannot* be free. Love cannot coexist with any kind of fear or doubt.

Now, how is this security achieved in the sphere of sex? Well, let us say that sexual union is a certain sort of gift which one person makes to another. It's very different from other gifts, and the difference lies in this: if I give you a present—say a book—the gift concerns us two and no one else. But when two people give sex to one another, they are not giving something *of their own* to each other. They are drawing, for their gift, on a vast human capital—the fact of sex which differentiates our bodies and relates us to that mystery of life which goes far beyond our own private thoughts and desires: the two people unite *in* something which they do not possess, and so there is always room for misunderstanding. They cannot be sure that it means the same thing for both of them. It *can* mean wildly different

60

things: for the boy, a pure personal passion; for the girl, a child, a house, a secure budget.

People have always known about this pitfall. They have coped with it in the following way. The act of sex involves the whole human community, and so we deliberately and openly call in the whole community to recognize our union. Thus we secure our union against our private misinterpretations. Thus and thus only, do we have free love. In this wonderful common language of marriage, in this high sacrament, the two can come together. The girl can learn to intend more than children and security, and the boy to intend more than romance.

Sex outside marriage

What is wrong with sex outside marriage? That is a question which our society is asking, with growing insistence. It is a good question, and demands a good answer.

What makes people feel that sex outside marriage is not always wrong? The easy answer is that the conscience of our society has gone dim. This is not an adequate answer. I think that what makes many young people feel that sex outside marriage need not be wrong, is a certain experience they have. It is a very important experience and, rightly understood and handled, it is a big step towards moral maturity. Let me try to desribe it. A young man knows, from his Catholic training, that he must turn his mind away from sexual self-interest, from sexual awareness in himself taken in isolation. Then he falls in love, or at least feels in love, and for the first time he experiences sexual self-awareness *in a completely different context*. It used to be a sort of *self*-indulgence. It is *now* part and parcel of a feeling for another person. Now what moral yardstick has he got for coping with this new experience? The one he was brought up on? That was framed for dealing with solitary experience of sex, so how can it be applied to an experience which is the very antithesis of solitude? On the other side, he is given no *social* principle of sexual morality, except the bare authoritative statement that sex with certain persons is wrong. And so he flounders between a boyhood morality no longer relevant and a manhood morality not yet to hand. He is like someone trying to make a good use of speech when all he has been told is that it's a bit cracked to talk to oneself. The truth of the matter is that this experience, far from being merely 'an occasion of sin', is someone *beginning* the discovery of a fact which, *completely* understood, is the whole basis of sexual morality: that sex is, through and through, a *social* reality. It is social in the sense that it brings two young people together, but it is *also* social in the wider and deeper sense that it involves the whole human community. It is this wider and deeper meaning of sex that is the whole and sole principle of sexual morality.

Following a sermon on sex

Overheard at the church door: 'It was a very peculiar sermon, so vague and inconclusive. He didn't come out clearly with the doctrine of the Church.'

Well, why should he? Don't you know it? Do you need reminding of it? Or do you think your brother needs reminding of it?

In our preaching, and in this book, we want to take a *fresh* look at things we know only too well, and not simply repeat the Church's teaching on them. On the question of sex outside marriage, for example, we want people, especially young people, to be able to enter into the Church's mind not only with their obedient wills but with their human feelings as well. It is very much the spirit of the present time to be dissatisfied with an authoritarian morality. We may deplore this spirit, but we cannot ignore it for it is part of us, whether we like it or not. And it is not wholly bad: it is evidence of a desire for a fuller and more meaningful moral life.

And so, in this matter, we want to show that extra-marital sex is not only something *forbidden*, but is something *unreal*— above all is something quite *different* from the free and full exercise of sex in marriage. The Church should not only be telling young people what is right and wrong. She should be showing young people how to become conscious of themselves, conscious that in spite of the blandishments of popularized sex, it is she and not it that holds the secret of a full life. It is the Church, and not the world, that is committed to the proposition that life is exciting.

But there's a snag to this approach, and we'd better face it. We are appealing to experience, and experience is a vastly rich and variegated thing. It cannot offer us conclusive proof. It offers us, instead, insight and understanding. But once a person has come to *appreciate* and understand how precious a thing is his life as a man, then he is far better disposed to commit it to the Church's keeping.

IX

MARRIAGE SERMONS

Michael and Margaret

THE FIRST thing God is recorded as having said about that extraordinary creature man, whom he had just created, was: 'It is not good for man to be alone.'

Hence, all unhappiness consists in being alone. A man who feels himself alone sees no purpose in life, no meaning. I was recently talking with a group of atheists who kept throwing at me all the horrible things that happen in the world. One of them was a Jew, and his parents had gone into Hitler's gas chambers. How, he said, could I believe in a God who let that sort of thing go on? Afterwards, a Catholic woman who had been present said to me: 'I felt just the same way about God for years, and drifted away from the Church. Then I met Bill, and everything was different.'

Yes indeed. Love is God's way of showing himself to us. To love, or be loved, and to be joined in marriage, is God's greatest gift to us. And in every gift, God gives himself.

Never forget this. Today God draws you out of your loneliness into the love that makes sense of your lives. Keep this love alive by faithfulness and trust and self-sacrifice, and you will be close to God. For you will then be living in the world he made, and not in the private world that selfish man makes for himself.

How little we were taught about God! We were brought up to think of him as a person easily offended, instead of seeing him as the meaning of our lives, the warm strong sunlight in which we grow together. It is in marriage that we come to understand him better, in whom we live and move and have our being.

Francis and Kathleen

It is written in the Bible that Adam and Eve, after the first sin, discovered that they were naked, and were ashamed. This does not mean what people seem to think. It does not mean that they saw in their bodies a tendency to evil. No, what they saw in their bodies, in their nature as man and woman, was God's design that they should give themselves completely to each other: and *this they could not do* because they had turned against God and become self-centred. *This* is what made them ashamed. They saw in their God-given bodily nature the emblem, the symbol, of a generosity and self-surrender of which they were no longer capable.

Christ has destroyed the sin of Adam, and brought man and woman together again. This is the glory of Christian marriage. But the old Adam is still strong in us, making us self-centred and reluctant to love. And this is the only sin against marriage: the refusal to love. Anyone who thinks that this makes it easier not to sin, anyone who thinks it is easy to love, has everything to learn.

Keep this thought before you as the programme of your married life. Love, and love alone, is required of you. It is enough, and it is much. May he who has planted the seed of love in your hearts bring it to fruition.

c

X

MIDNIGHT, 1967

I SPEAK of you. I speak of me. I speak because I cannot be silent. I speak for man. It is man who speaks.

I have a past, in which an infant howls in the darkness, a man is nailed to a cross, and a bunch of outlandish individuals rush around speaking in unfamiliar tongues. I have a present, where I struggle to know and to be known, the struggle in which we are all involved, the seemingly hopeless struggle towards the light. I have a future, where the struggle ends in nothing but light.

These three, the Christ-past, the Christ-present, and the Christ-future, are all one. I cannot validly know the infant who stretches his hands out to the cross, except as forcing *my* hands to the embrace of others, to the suffering that this causes, and to the light that is its promised end. We cannot enshrine the Christ of Bethlehem. His nakedness is either ours or it is not God's revelation at all. And what is our nakedness? It is our willed exposure to those who do not know us and to those who know us too well for our liking. It is that 'love which suffers all things' of which the Apostle speaks. It is our life. It is the mess we are in, the seemingly impossible tangle of relationships. It is the one thing we want above all to escape and cannot. It is what will be. And it is Christ, born in nakedness, speaking out of nakedness, hung naked on a cross, and established in power, who will not let me forget what it is to be man, who forces me along the one really painful way which is the way of growth.

Throughout the Christian centuries, men have sought for

ways of proving the truth of the Christian religion. But in the end I come back simply to this: that Christ will not let me forget what it is to be man. Do this: remember me: remember ... I don't know why it is that he alone forces my destiny upon me. I don't know why it is that when I think of all men and then think of him I am forced to say: this is the heart. This is me. This is what cannot be escaped. This is what must grow and change or be lost eternally.

That is the lesson of this night. It is *our* night, in which we wake and shiver and tremble before an uncertain future. And his birth is that miracle whereby all, absolutely all that may happen to us, is embraced, and in the embrace we know joy and peace. Choose *that* peace and no other. Let nothing divert us from the peace from which nothing is excluded. Let nothing make us afraid. Let us courageously apply the following test to all that we have been taught to believe: if it makes us fearful and doubtful of ourselves, if it makes us small and timid, then it is not of Christ. For too long we have learned of Christ from small and cautious men, who could not trust us and sought to mould us to a pattern of rules of conduct and religious observances. That, they said, was Christ. It is not. Christ is you and me, here and now, knowing that the way forward is in love alone. Believe in yourself and in the life that will not let you stand still. Believe in man. God does. Of this fact we have the most embarrassing evidence. For

> the Word was made flesh,
> he lived among us,
> and we saw his glory.

PART TWO

XI

'HE THAT HAS EARS TO HEAR'

Do we hear?

ANYONE WHO HAS TRIED to explain something to a group of people whose reactions he is able to assess knows that there are several levels of comprehension. Some follow all that is said and actually jump ahead of the teacher—maybe even see more than the teacher; some just manage to keep abreast of the explanation; others do not quite see the point at present, but catch up later on when they have had time for reflection; and some never understand what is being talked about. For these last (presuming they do not actually go to sleep) the actual *words* are all heard and any diagrams on the blackboard or pictures are seen, but the *significance* of what was seen and heard is entirely lost.

In the matter of religion, which is nothing other than an awareness of the significance of life, the only real teacher is life itself. We all learn various subjects at school and often afterwards too, and we need teachers to learn from. But religion gives us a broader understanding and a unified view of what cannot be factually 'put across' as a theorem in geometry can. So in religious matters the teacher (and all of us are in a teaching position at some time or other) must always be conscious that he is a *fellow-seeker* with those he teaches. Otherwise he would fall under the heavy condemnation of those who seek to be called Rabbi, Teacher or Father by men.

Life is known in experience, and those who learn from it fall into the same rough categories as pupils in a class: some surge ahead, always anticipating what is around the next corner;

some just manage to keep up with the growth in experience; some are confused but manage to catch up; and finally, some merely drift along, seeing and hearing the same things as the others but never beginning to make sense of it at all.

'He that has ears to hear, let him hear.'

Urgent concern

If you strip the Christian message, in terms of practical application, to its core, it can sound pretty obvious: that it is necessary to spend ourselves in the service of others, that this is the only way to happiness, the only way to salvation. This, as someone I was speaking to the other day said, sounds common sense.

But although it *is* common sense, and this is what Christian morality is about, we must do far more than *assent* to this proposition. It's not merely a question of saying 'Oh yes, I see this and I'm going to apply it in my own life as well as I can.' Something much more is needed: there has to be a *concern* in the very deepest sense—a concern which *disturbs* us, urges us to do something. We need to see with clarity the terrifying predicament of man in his present situation: the lack of concern for others; the lack of love, and so the lack of peace; the enormous danger that hangs over our heads. And when we do see this, we are bound to feel a terrible sense of urgency, because not enough people see it for the community to which we belong to be transformed in the only way that can save it. Perhaps if we saw with sufficient clarity, we should find ourselves too weak to bear the vision. Yet a degree of this insight into the failure of our generation is essential if we are even to begin to have a specifically Christian outlook on life. Such was the insight of the prophets of the Old Testament; it caused them to say things which risked their lives; it was the insight of the apostles, of St Paul, and above all, of course, of Christ himself.

And surely this is the meaning of the cross: that once we have seen, we feel an enormous responsibility for the generation to which we belong—a responsibility that compels us to go on, in the face of any opposition.

Reflective action

How is this urgent sense of responsibility to be achieved? Not by reflection, thought or prayer alone. No amount of thinking will solve the problems of our world. Pure reflection will simply build up a ready-made solution in a world that is make-believe, a world of abstract thought, which doesn't in fact exist at all. And when Christians (or any one else for that matter) present the world with a purely intellectual solution, it is just treated with contempt by those who have to apply themselves practically to the problem.

Yet, again, the insight we need cannot be achieved merely by action. If we simply bludgeon on 'doing good' without reflecting on the point of it all, then the effort is soon lost in confusion, without any direction.

True insight (found in the Jews and continued among Christians when they are true to themselves), is insight into the *wholeness* of man: not man, consisting of body and soul as two separate principles, but man as *one*. Not man, a body which acts and a soul which reflects, but one reflective doer. And this is enormously important, because human experience gives us a realization of our wholeness, teaches us to act reflectively.

It isn't a question of thinking first, coming to a conclusion, and then putting the conclusion into practice; nor of rushing blindly into action and then rationalizing what one has done. It's a matter of living, in which our engagement with the world and the problems we have to face day by day, gives rise to a deeper understanding of those problems. And at the same time reflection deepens the meaning of our action and stimulates us to further action.

This, I think, helps us make more sense of what we mean by the priesthood of the whole people of God, which is all Christians. Priesthood is mediation. It is not mediation to offer an intellectual solution to a problem without actually *doing* anything about it. That is simply disinterested advice. The Christian is one who cares to the depths of his being about the need of the world; cares about the salvation of the world, its fulfilment in God. And precisely this is a priestly function, when his caring means not only understanding, not merely seeing, but at the same time urges him to acting, doing all that can be done, realizing that because one has seen, because one is aware, one is forced, in the very process of understanding, to give one's whole self in the service of mankind.

Adding a cubit to your stature

Physical growth comes to an end, but growth in maturity should never stop—we should continue to mature throughout the whole of our lives.

If we look back to the stages we have passed through in our growth, and ask what has made us grow, we find ourselves somewhat at a loss. It's not only that we're not responsible for being born and that we didn't bring ourselves up. Even since we reached adulthood (when we should still be maturing), we

know that development has often occurred because of particular
decisive events, problems and difficulties that have cropped up
in our life, *through* which we have come to a deeper understand-
standing and consequently to a greater maturity. But we have not
planned even these really decisive events: they have just
happened.

To be aware of this is to be aware of *grace*. So to be open
to growth in maturity (which is of course the opposite of developing a set, inflexible outlook) is to cooperate with grace; to
be open to change in ourselves. But this is as much as we can do:
we can only be open to change in ourselves; we cannot actually
cause ourselves to grow. As our Lord said to the crowds 'Which
of you by taking thought can add one cubit to your stature?'

It follows that we are not able to *give* maturity to another
person. He must see for himself, must open himself to change.

So those who are involved in helping other people to mature
(and that should be all of us at one time or another) are presented with an enormous problem. We can all see the need to
reach the specifically Christian stage of maturity which is self-
giving in love rather than self-centredness in fear. Yet we
can't confer this state on ourselves or on others to order—however much we may want to. It requires a fundamental change in
the self. Nothing is more awful than somebody *acting as if* they
loved, when you know that in point of fact they do not and
their act is *only* an act of the will. Our job is to *dispose for* the
gift of growth. We ourselves must seek, and encourage others
to seek, so that seeking we may find. We must not so much provide answers as raise questions. In this way we dispose for that
grace by which we can all grow, as St Paul puts it, 'to mature
manhood, even the measure of the stature of the totality of
Christ'.

XII

THE OLD LAW AND THE NEW

Responsibility and freedom

WE ARE FAIRLY WELL acquainted with the fact that the Scribes and Pharisees were the target for Our Lord's criticism—that he was rebelling against the outlook of the accepted leaders of Judaism. Why did he?

The Pharisees, at their best, were a group of Jews who believed in and practised a rigorous fidelity to the laws of God, according to the spirit of the psalmist who said, 'Your laws are my delight and my counsellors.' Theirs was a rigid and austere way of life based on total obedience, in the confidence that such obedience would be rewarded, perhaps in this life, but certainly after death at the resurrection. At their worst the Pharisees had a merely legalistic attitude to human behaviour which resulted in the toleration of any behaviour which did not technically break the law. And for all of them, their creed meant despising those who did not observe the law in all its detail.

Pharisaism gave no room for manoeuvre within the law, no room for the moral responsibility or freedom to decide in a given situation that the right course might involve breaking the letter of the law. This was why our Lord clashed with them over the matter of sabbath-keeping, saying: 'The sabbath was made for man, not man for the sabbath.' And the same principle, of course, applies to the whole law, not merely to sabbath observance.

St Paul, speaking as one who has progressed from a Jewish to a Christian view of life and law, has a great deal to say about all this. He had been a Pharisee, and had clearly tried to live up to Pharisaism at its best. But he found that in fact its ideal could not really be lived up to: 'Wretched man that I am . . . that which I ought to do I do not; and that which I would not do, that I do.' He observed the persistent tendency to slip into a legalistic frame of mind, dodging the spirit of the law while sticking to its letter.

In one passage St Paul sees the old law (as lived by the best of the Pharisees) as a kind of *tutor* for men while they were still children. But the time was coming when men must grow up, and 'put away childish things'. He could think like the Pharisees no longer, he had grown out of their attitude, and he saw that all those who 'have ears to hear' what Christ had to say must necessarily do likewise.

We all know that young children (even if they are not in fact obedient) think in terms of *'What am I allowed to do?'* rather than 'What is best for me to do?' But as they grow older, they develop the desire to think out and decide for themselves what is right.

The person who does not mature in this way remains a child, and cannot grasp the fundamental point about Christianity: the exercise of freedom for the individual becomes Christian when conscience is dominated by the law of love, when he does right not only because he is told to (if he is told to), but because he sees for himself what he ought to do.

As Christians we are not born into slavery but into freedom, not into subservience to an arbitrary law, but into a free commitment involving our own responsibility and mature judgement—the 'freedom by which Christ has made us free'.

On taking sides

A passage from the prophecy of Jeremiah reads: 'Blessed

be the man who trusts in the Lord. . . . He shall be as a tree that is planted by the waters, that spreads out its roots towards the moisture: and it shall not fear when the heat comes.'

In this passage we find some of the basic human images, images which seem to be *the* basis only to anyone who has made a study of primitive religion. Water, the source of life; fertility. The tree, found in almost all mythologies about the origins of man and of the world, as it is found in the bible both at the beginning, with the tree of the knowledge of good and evil, and at the end, with the tree in the Apocalypse that stands at the juncture of the waters of life. And the imagery is always the same, in whatever mythology: the tree is rooted in the earth, it grows on the earth and stretches out its branches towards its fulfilment, towards the heavens. This is a vital symbol of all human hopes and desires: that we may grow, and that we may grow firmly rooted.

We hear a great deal these days about 'progressives' and 'conservatives', and it is rather important to keep very clearly in our minds what exactly we mean by these labels, to avoid misusing them. We need to beware of attaching ourselves to either *camp*, of labelling ourselves either conservative or progressive. Once we think of ourselves as either one or the other we shall certainly begin to miss seeing the point of the issues that face us. The snag about progressives and anti-conservatives is that they tend towards revolution, towards overthrowing and devaluing everything that has gone before. The snag about conservatives is that they tend to freeze things as they always have been, to prevent growth, to keep things stagnant.

But the true progressive sees a tremendous value in the past. He knows that what he is, and what the world is, and what the Church is, and what is essential in many human situations, is so because it has grown out of the past. The past has gone to make us what we are now. This is true of us all individually, and it's true of every community there ever was. We cannot throw our past overboard and say that all this was meaningless, because if we do that we are saying that we are meaningless.

No, we must value the past, but as the basis of what we are now, the roots from which we can go further, from which we can grow.

And therefore the true progressive is in fact the only true conservative. He is the only *true* conservative because he values the past, realistically, for what it is and for what it means. But he does not try to cling to it and to live in the past once it is over. The past is the ingredient of the present and the clue to the future. It is the roots from which our present hope puts out new shoots; and so long as we allow this, then we shall be in a much better position to see what needs to be done and where we ought to go.

XIII

CHRIST THE REVOLUTIONARY:
YESTERDAY AND TODAY

THE ATTITUDE OF THE chief priests in the gospels strikes us as
very strange: they admit that Jesus works miracles and that
therefore he will have a large following, and yet they want to
suppress him. We might have expected that they, if anyone,
would have recognized the signs Jesus did, and would have
been prepared to take the risk involved in letting him go on
preaching. Of course, the truth is that they feared that if he did
go on, the Romans would crush what they would take to be
a rebellion—and that would be altogether the end of any kind
of Jewish state.

I don't think it's quite fair to say that the chief priests only
cared about themselves and their own position of honour which
was bolstered up by the Romans. They certainly *did* care about
that, but their most powerful motive for fearing Christ was
that they couldn't cope with the possibility that the politico-
religious structure of the Jewish state might be swept away. The
thought filled them with a desperate fear of the unknown.

I think most of us can understand this feeling—because we
all depend more or less heavily (in practice) on the con-
tinuity and stability of our institutions. However much we may
recognize a need for change (and we may even be actively en-
gaged in trying to bring it about), we are still reluctant to see the
old world as we have known it passing away. We tend to regret
the changing face of things as we have known them, because we
cling to the security (even though it is a false security) of what
we have known and regarded as permanent. This is why many

violently resist the changes in the Church—because the Church has been made by fearful men into a comforting mother to whom we could run with our troubles, instead of a force of revolution in the staid world of men.

The real significance of what the chief priests did is that they chose the *known* situation which, though dull and uninspired, gave a certain sense of comfort; and they rejected the inspired approach of Christ in spite of all its exciting possibilities, because of the unknown quantities and dangers that might lie in it. In other words, they played safe.

Looking back on it two thousand years later, we can see the thing in better perspective. We know that in fact about thirty years later the Romans destroyed Jerusalem anyway, and we know also that this helped the growth of the Christian idea. The Christian idea took the Jewish idea forward, while Judaism remained a religion isolated from the world around it.

It is therefore all the more inexcusable that we should allow *ourselves* to follow the 'safe' line of the chief priests, trying to preserve our institutions (and with them our sense of security) at the price of stifling the movement of the Spirit. We must seek change and growth. These will come anyway—but if we try to resist rather than to lead and guide we shall find ourselves left behind, an unimportant backwater of no significance.

XIV

THE EXPERIENCE OF FAITH

HOW MUCH difference experience makes in day-to-day things!
You may learn quite a lot about playing football, or mending a
light fuse or running a household, or anything else you care
to mention, simply by reading about it or by watching how
it is done. But until you actually *do* it yourself the knowledge
remains theoretical not practical, and you are only an observer,
not a participant.

St John, reflecting on the events of Jesus' life, death and
resurrection, makes this remark: 'Whatever is born of God
transforms the world—our *faith*.' And he gives as his reason
for setting down the gospel: 'That you may believe that Jesus
is the Christ the Son of God; and that, believing, you may
have *life* in his name.' Elsewhere he says that we should have
life, and *have it more abundantly*.

Yet what many people call faith, or 'having the faith', does
not seem to give them abundant life at all. On the contrary, it
often seems to deaden them to life by fixing them in a rigid
outlook, incapable of development. We cannot have full knowledge of what John means by faith, which is to transform the
world and give more abundant life, without experiencing it.

No matter how accurately we can recite the details of the
events recorded in the gospels, or how firmly we are convinced that they did happen as recorded, unless there is something *in our own experience* which has a transforming and
life-giving effect on us, we have not faith. However much we
rehearse the *arguments* in favour of the resurrection, unless

there is a happening in ourselves, a real change, we have not true faith. Faith is not a thing we can give ourselves—but we can and must seek it.

St Thomas the apostle would not believe in the resurrection until he had seen the physical evidence for himself; he is rebuked for lack of faith. But it was not just that he refused to believe the facts reported to him—no one can be expected to accept virtually incredible evidence without good reason; that would be mere gullibility. No, Thomas's failure was deeper than that.

I think that to understand it we need to think of this incident alongside the appearance to the two disciples on the road to Emmaus. Then, you remember, the disciples told how, while they walked along and listenened to this apparent stranger expounding the scriptures, their 'hearts burned within' them. They came to an enlightenment; to a new understanding of life itself. The Messiah, they realized, *had* to suffer, because he had to reveal to man his own nature and the meaning of his life—and the meaning of life is that truth is known in love; that loving is giving and not keeping; that to love we have to spend ourselves, and in so doing we achieve ourselves; that in order to live we have to die.

This was what Thomas had not learned. It is something to believe it. We may hear the words and yet fail to understand them. That is why we are called upon to seek.

Faith and evidence

There are times when one cannot avoid being astonished by the literal-mindedness of the apostles. You find it in St Peter and his question about forgiving a man seven times; in James and John asking for seats of honour in the kingdom; in the apostles thinking, because Jesus said he had bread to eat that they knew not of, that someone had been giving him food. This simplicity recurs again and again. And it recurs in St Thomas's refusing to believe in the resurrection until he had concrete evidence of the risen body.

We ought not to misjudge St Thomas. In point of fact *none* of the disciples, immediately after the resurrection, believed without also seeing the risen Christ in some way—except St John who, you remember, coming to the tomb 'went in, and he saw and believed; for as yet they did not know the scripture that he must rise from the dead'.

And even John had the empty tomb for evidence, though this was scarcely adequate in itself. The truth is that there *must* be some evidence to justify faith; it cannot and ought not to be found in 'signs and wonders', but rather in a more fundamental human experience: our awareness that the growth of this world is purposeful and that there is a meaning in the development of individual men and communities, so that whatever death is, it cannot nullify the growth that preceded it. Precisely this experience was what Christ was trying to communicate to the apostles, and it was this above all that should have enabled them to believe—and not the fact that they saw an apparition, however solid.

Oddly enough, evidence that is *too* literal and concrete actually *hinders* faith in those who are too literal-minded, because it encourages a concentration on the astonishing and the miraculous that is more pagan than Christian.

So we'd be wrong to think of Christ's reproof to St Thomas as suggesting that he ought to have believed blindly without reason; rather, they are a warning to him, to all the apostles, and to all time, against seeing in the resurrection only an extraordinary phenomenon, while failing to see that it is around us and has meaning for us here and now.

XV

ADVENT NOTES

'Dew from above'

IN THE Office for Advent the following passage from one of the psalms is constantly recurring: 'Let the heavens send down dew from above; let the earth open and bring forth a saviour.' Read that phrase again: Christ is the gift of God, the dew from above: this is an idea with which we are all perfectly familiar. But by itself it is very misleading, and it is completed at once with another theme: Christ springs out of the *earth*, from this world.

We are encumbered in our thinking as a people, as a Church, with an individualism that tends to make nonsense of Christianity. We say something like this: 'Christ was God, as an isolated individual, and we, as isolated individuals, having passed a test in this life, are given eternal life still as individuals, and continue as such with Christ after our death.'

If we are to make sense of Christianity it's vital that we come to see the whole world process as one creative act of God. Christ must be seen as growing from this world, the product, if you like, of evolution (taking the widest meaning of the word: the growth of the world as a whole). He comes also from heaven, since all growth is a gift of God. Christ grew out of the world; he grew out of it and was not just injected into it as something alien, from outside. In Christ we must grow out of our isolated individualism into the corporate personality which is to be the fulfilment of all things. This doesn't mean we lose our personality. Isolated in ourselves we are nothing. We lose nothing by forgoing our *individuality*; only in love and service of others, which realizes the kingdom of heaven (the personality of God) among us, do we realize our own personality.

'A shoot from the stump of Jesse'

In an important prophecy in the book of Isaiah, we get a very clear looking-forward to the coming of the Messiah: he is to be a flowering of that growing tree whose root is Jesse, the father of David. Too frequently we tend to see Christ as an individual who might just as well have been born to any woman God cared to choose at any old time in the world's history. It's this sort of thinking that lies behind the age-old objection to Christianity, found even in the earliest times, that if salvation depends on Christ, why on earth wasn't he born earlier? And the same thinking makes it very hard for Christians to find a satisfactory answer to this objection.

No! Christ as an individual was rooted in the history of his people, the Jews, and the process of God becoming man and of man becoming God *began* not with his birth, but with the beginning of creation itself. He was and is the final flowering of a tree rooted in the very origins of the universe, a tree which grew through evolution to mankind and then through the Jewish people, through King David and finally through Mary his mother. The way in which God is redeeming the world is the way in which he is creating the world, and he, God, is himself being realized in his creation.

And that's not all. We think of ourselves, too, as being self-contained individuals; but we too, like Christ, have our origins in the very foundations of the world. We do not take our *origin* from our parents: they are part of us and we are part of them. If we are to begin to 'know ourselves', as the modern philosophers like to put it, we must first understand this: that we are inextricably bound up with one another and with our ancestors and with all creation, part of the one universe with its single purpose which is the creative activity of God. So we are one also with Christ, in whom the purpose of God was first fully realized in an individual man—the purpose that is finally to be realized in the whole creation. To be aware of this, even dimly, is to be aware of the cosmic significance of Christ—and it is to be a Christian in more than name.

'The spirit of the Lord shall rest upon him'

Isaiah saw the Messiah as having the fulness of wisdom and understanding, courage, justice, knowledge: all the qualities needed, we may say with hindsight, for the full Christian understanding of love.

The prophet also envisages that this man would have a lasting impact on the whole world. Isaiah lived in a time of political confusion, war and social injustice on a colossal scale. It's easy to imagine many people of his day saying 'Well, this is all very fine, but it's difficult to imagine anyone ever having all these qualities, ever being so impressive that he could make a real impact on the impossible situation which we're faced with now.' These would be the pessimists, the people who judged the future in terms of the present; to them, Isaiah's prophecy must have seemed purely idealistic, something that could never really happen.

And yet Isaiah's faith was justified; even those who do not accept Christianity in its entirety would agree that Christ was a most impressive man, and could scarcely deny that he *has* made a colossal impact on the world. So he certainly fulfilled the hope of Isaiah.

Today we are in a different situation. Christians look forward to a time when the impact made on the world by Christ as an individual will produce the fruits of universal peace and unity in love. Today, as in the time of Isaiah, it is difficult to see how this can ever come about, even though we acknowledge that this man who was also God was so impressive that he could change people with whom he came in contact. And yet it seems very far-fetched, very idealistic, to believe that the fulfilment of the world, on the pattern in which Christ was fulfilled, can ever be realized. Yet Christian faith demands that we should believe this. And Christian faith is not blind faith. It must be founded on experience.

For the apostles, faith in this future fulfilment *was* founded on their present experience in the time that followed Pentecost when they were united in common purpose and bound together in love. And likewise, in any age, such faith is possible only for those who already have a partial experience (not of course a complete one) of the reality they hope for, who have some experience of unity in common purpose. This can and must become a compelling thing, urging them to make their experience more widespread.

This is what Christ meant when he said, 'The kingdom of heaven is among you.' And St John: 'We proclaim to you the *eternal* life which was with the Father and which was made to us [in experience, that is]. That which we have *seen* and *heard* we proclaim also to you, so that you may have fellowship with us.'

The coming of Christ

There is a great sense of looking-forward about Advent. The liturgy is full of such expressions as 'O Lord, come, and do not delay; loosen the bonds of your people'; 'Send forth thy power and come among us'; 'Let the earth open and bring forth a saviour', drawn largely from the Old Testament texts which look forward to the birth of a Messiah, a descendant of the great and almost legendary King David, who would come and put right what was wrong with the world—prophecies by men who, despite the steadily deteriorating social and political situation, pinned their faith on this future leader who would vindicate his people in the power of God.

From this point of view the whole spirit of Advent is Old Testament, expressed in words which were originally words of hope in a fulfilment still to come. But what should this spirit of Advent mean today?

If you turn on the radio on Christmas Eve you may hear the Carol Service from King's College Chapel, Cambridge, with its time-honoured bidding prayer; 'Let us now go even unto Bethlehem and see the great things that have come to pass there in these days.'

Is this what we have come to? Are we only playing a game of make-believe, *pretending*, for the fun of it, that Christ is to be born in the future? We sing carols and have a crib and go to the midnight Mass: and it does almost seem as though that's all we're doing—pretending.

You ask, 'Why shouldn't we be a bit sentimental about Christmas if we want to be?' There's no harm, certainly, in dwelling on the fairy-tale element in the circumstances of Christ's birth two thousand years ago. Not, that is, so long as our attention is not exclusively turned back to the past event without any reference to now.

But what has the spirit of Advent, the eager straining forward in faith to a *future* event, to do with us now? The prophets of the Old Testament expressed their hope for a great deliverer in a time of social injustice, dishonesty, constant threat of war, a time when even the existence of the nation was in danger, and there was a lack of unity among the people, constant bickering and argument, so that their future was imperilled by their own weakness as well as by outside foes. Yet the prophets were optimistic enough and had faith enough to hope for a happy outcome in the end.

Their faith was *not* a blind faith. In spite of all they knew to be wrong, they had experienced in their lives mercy and justice and love even in the face of infidelity: and experiencing this, they *knew* (though 'through a glass, darkly') that not only were these the *only* true values, but also that they were the most powerful and must prevail in the end.

The hope of the prophets was finally realized in one man in whom love was made flesh: a man who had the secret of life and of death, because he *was love*, he was God. We hope, too, but our hope will not again be fulfilled in a single man (history doesn't repeat itself). It will be fulfilled in the final triumph of love as the only true value, the true *life* of this world. This implies the unification of all men, not under compulsion but freely, in love—which is what we mean by saying we shall be one in Christ.

But our faith and our hope are not blind either—not, that is, where they are genuine and compelling. Many of us have personal experience of becoming one, in love, in a common purpose—most of us, perhaps. Without some experience of this, a living faith is impossible. But when such unity is a matter of experience, however confused, it becomes possible for us to 'read the signs of the times', to know what our Lord meant when he said 'the kingdom of God is among you' and 'when two or three are gathered together in my name, there am I in the midst of them'. *Then* we no longer look back nostalgically to a past incarnation, nor blindly forwards to a remote second coming: our Advent becomes *now*. We come to know that we ourselves are undergoing change, and we have a sense of an impending transformation both in ourselves individually and in our society.

'The Lord is near to all that call upon him in truth.'

XVI

THE UNITY OF CHRISTIANS

Individual and community

WE ARE ALL AWARE that in isolation we are incomplete; only in unity with others do we find some sort of greater wholeness. In any group—a football team, a ship's crew, a family—we know that the person who tries to detach himself and act regardless of the others not only harms the effectiveness of the group, but in the long run harms himself as well. None of us likes a selfish man; it is the man who genuinely loves others who is himself lovable. This not only gives us an idea, as if by analogy, of what the Church is; in experiencing it, we actually *know* the Church.

St Paul lists various particular functions within the community (prophecy, ministry, teaching, giving, ruling, showing mercy); these overlap with one another and are not limited to the sort of functions (like ruling) that a particular person can be appointed to do. In fact *all* members of the community have some function in Paul's sense: they all have something to give. He goes on to say, 'Let love be without dissimulation.' This, unless limited to friendships between individuals who already naturally like one another, can only possibly become a reality in a community where all play their part with a sense of common purpose. 'Love' that is a pretence (an act of will based on the precept that we ought to love, but without any feeling) is hopeless; but when there is a common purpose the most unlikely people find themselves united—this is the 'charity of brotherhood' of which St Paul speaks.

Again, he says we should be 'of one mind one with another'

—an idea some regard not only as impracticable but even as un-
desirable, on the grounds that it would take away the individual's personality. Genuine unity of mind does not do this:
only through a fully developed personality can this kind of
unity be attained. Think of the cells of the human body (as
St Paul does elsewhere): the *more* varied the component parts
(the more developed their individual characteristics) the more
effective is the group they compose—so long as that group is
not divided against itself.

Today there is a strong movement towards Christian unity.
Any divisions within the human community are destructive
(not only ecclesiastical ones). And where there are divisions,
it means that however large a group may be it forms only a part
of the whole, and for wholeness needs the rest.

The 'rightness' of the Catholic Church is limited by this
inescapable fact: it does not and cannot mean that the Church
possesses everything it could desire. 'Catholic' means 'universal'; but in so far as the Church is only partial it fails to be
catholic.

The Church, as we say in the creed, is one, holy, catholic and
apostolic—but if we are careless in the way we apply these
words, we shall find ourselves speaking a manifest lie with
appalling arrogance. Certainly we do believe, as St Peter puts
it, that the Church is 'the pillar and the ground of truth', but
we must not oversimplify this so that we fail to find any good
outside the Church. To do so would be to commit the one
unforgivable sin of calling evil that which is good.

Unity of all Christians

We must understand that the whole of Christian experience,
thought and teaching, is directed to the unifying of men into one
whole, into the Christ that is to be: 'That we may all grow up

into the measure of the stature of the totality of Christ.' All dogma and all moral teaching is in some way connected with this—and there are no exceptions.

This is why early Christian writers spoke of the Church as consisting of all mankind: the Church exists for *this* end, that mankind should be one in God; and therefore it cannot be perfect (fulfilled) until *that* end is achieved.

But, for all that, we know that the solution to the world's problems lies in particular in the Christian tradition—so St Peter calls the Church 'the pillar and the ground of truth'. But let's not get this wrong. We must not imagine that we have the truth ready to hand, and can hand it out to anyone prepared to ask us. We know perfectly well that not one of us can provide a universal answer like this even for ourselves—so how can we expect to give it to others?

We live in a world of *becoming*; therefore the Christian message is not a static, ready-made *answer*. It is a pointer based on a (limited) experience—experience of unity achieved in common purpose with the bond of love, such as Christ demonstrated and taught in his own life. It *points* towards a solution, and it does so in the changing human community that we call the Church.

Now, the pattern of development in the community is roughly this: it has had a glimpse of the significance of the universe and all that is in it, but because of the limitations (the childishness, we may say) of men, this vision is constantly being reduced to a system—a 'religion' which bears all the marks of being an exclusive *cult*. There are always some within the community who know that this is *not* what the community is really meant to be: these people are the leaven in the lump. Sometimes these prophets (for that is what they are) manage to get what they see accepted by the rulers in the Church, but sometimes they fail. The failure will be due partly to their own inadequacy, of course, but also to the inadequacy, the lack of vision, in the Church itself. And so a heresy may be born, and lead to a schism.

The point I want to make is this: when a group breaks away from the main body of Christians (forgetting degrees of blame for the moment), that group tends to take with it a very important truth. The Catholic Church *reacts* against the group, and also against its beliefs and so is crippled by the blow.

The search for Christian unity will not *fail* simply because it does not produce a single *organization*. If we approach other Christians with a will to *learn* from them, we Catholics will begin to understand our own faith more deeply, and the deficiencies in our presentation of it to others will begin to be remedied.

Rome and the East

There is an important lesson to be learned from the history of the relationship between the Latin Roman Catholic Church and the several Churches of the East. Some of these groups broke away from the main body of Christians at a very early date, on theological issues which no longer seem to have any influence on the thinking of ordinary Christians within them. But the final break between Rome and Constantinople in 1054, when both sides excommunicated one another, came as the culmination of a gradual estrangement between the two groups that really had nothing to do with genuine beliefs, but sprang from a distrust of the other side's way of going about things. In other words, it was largely due to the assumption (on both sides) that truth can be clearly expressed in words, and in only one set of words.

This is surely a fatal mistake. Anyone who has tried to convey on paper a profound experience that has changed his whole life, must know how impossible it is. Take the obvious example of the first time you become so aware of another person that you 'fall in love'. Can you possibly hope to explain the commitment you feel to someone who has not had such an experience? Of course you can't. And if you cannot, why suppose that the way you do in fact express it is the only way it can be expressed? Look at all the love poetry that has been written—there are about as many ways of expressing the case as there are poets who have made the attempt. Nor is it surprising that those who want to write about love turn to poetry: the experience of love cannot be put in a *logical* way, so that they turn to images to make their point.

When a man really comes to see what Christianity is all about, it is very like falling in love. His vision takes hold of him and will not leave him alone, it gives meaning to the whole of his life. Yet so often people want to turn Christianity into a kind of scientific explanation of the world. But you can't get to Christianity by philosophy and reasoning alone (though these have their place): it is an experience, and cannot adequately be expressed in words. That is why our Lord spoke in parables.

Perhaps the mutual revocation of the 1054 excommunication of Rome and Constantinople will prove the prelude to a more realistic acceptance of the fact that Christianity cannot be reduced to words or propositions neatly set out on paper. If it does, then perhaps a way is beginning to open towards an external unity that would have seemed impossible even a few years ago.

The English experience

Because there is no single way to express the Christian experience we all need to learn from the experience of others.

What does this mean in relation to the ecumenical situation in England? Obviously in a short space I can't begin to do justice to the various Christian bodies in this country, but there are one or two points that are worth making.

It's very important to realize in the first place that the non-Roman Catholics in England can't be lumped together into one group and labelled 'Protestants'. The history of the situation is roughly this. The Church of England, the *Ecclesia Anglicana*, was the name originally used by the pre-Reformation Church in England, which was in communion with Rome. There's been no change of name. The break with Rome was not based on any doctrinal issue in the first instance, but on a desire for greater freedom from the centralized authority of Rome, which was heavily dominated by political interests. There were all sorts of less worthy motives, of course, but the issue was not a doctrinal one. Henry VIII, for all his personal faults (and none of us are in a position to throw stones at individuals for their personal faults), never departed from his Catholic faith, and had no intention of allowing the Church of England to do so (though things worked out differently in the event).

In what proved to be the final settlement under Elizabeth I, the aim was not to establish a Reformation Church like the ones on the continent, but to find a formula which would include what were by that time very diverse beliefs, ranging from Catholic to Protestant, all within the one national Church: so it was all rather vague, but not Protestant in the accepted sense. And to this day you will find within the Church of England all shades of belief, from pro-papal Catholic to very anti-papal 'evangelical'.

The other non-Roman Catholic groups in this country—I speak really of England, the Scots Presbyterians being in a different situation—are breakaways not from Catholicism but from Anglicanism, and they all stand for something quite definite, something important which they didn't find in the Church of England (but which at the time they wouldn't have found in the Catholic Church).

In working for the unity of Christians, it doesn't do to say, 'How can we hope to negotiate with Christian bodies that don't even know what they believe themselves?' The point is that we don't want to *negotiate* at all: what we want to do is to learn from each other's experience. If one day union becomes possible, that'll be fine; but it's not the immediate point of our contacts.

It isn't possible to give more than an indication of what we can learn from these groups, but here are a few suggestions: the Anglicans seem to reveal, above all, a decentralization of the Church, an attempt to achieve a *common* view rather than accept without question, without thinking for oneself, the views of the authorities; the Congregationalists and Presbyterians seem to reveal the *local Church* as a genuine community: the elders who rule the local Church are from that Church and not appointed from outside; the Baptists show us *adult* commitment, which is why they baptize their members as adults, at a time when they decide for themselves that they do want to become Christians; Methodists, though I'm afraid this was more striking earlier in their history, reveal to us enthusiasm, and to this day they stand for a concern with social justice, and for the fellowship of Christians.

All these things are recognizably Christian; and yet we must, if we're honest, admit that Catholicism has tended to play them down—sometimes to forget them altogether.

So let us try to learn by being open to the insights of others, and not be like the 'Nowhere Man' in the Beatles' song, who 'sees only what he wants to see'.

The European experience

The Protestant reformers undoubtedly saw something in Christianity which the Church in their day had obscured, and the sad history of division and mutual recrimination is due to fault on both sides and not only on the part of Luther, Calvin and Zwingli.

D

I want to develop a train of thought arising from much more recent events; the modern Ecumenical Movement began in Europe. The Abbé Paul Couturier, a French priest, devoted his life to drawing together those who found themselves divided by different Christian traditions. This movement started well before the Second World War, and was sparked off by Couturier's work on behalf of the Russian Orthodox refugees from Marxist Russia.

The really great impetus to ecumenism was occasioned, oddly enough, by the activities of the German Nazi party. It happened like this: the Nazis, inspired by racialism and a philosophy that was radically unchristian, anti-Christian, broke up the old order. Once the Second World War got under way their influence extended over practically the whole continent of Europe; *resistance* to the Nazis, both in Germany and outside it, came from men and women whose concern was to fight the tyranny of evil. Although they held very different religious positions— there were Catholics, Protestants, Jews, Communists, atheists —they had in common the desire for freedom and tolerance that is essentially Christian. This united them into a common cause, and united them at a much deeper level than one of simple agreement about dogmas. It was a *felt* unity, an experienced unity. The fact was borne in upon them that what they had in common was vastly more important than what separated them: so it turned upside down the old attitudes of suspicion between Christians, in which the tendency was to emphasize what separated and to disregard what was held in common. It was out of this experience that post-war ecumenism was able to develop.

We can learn two things about our own situation from this. Firstly, we in England never suffered the break-up of the old order, the turning upside down of all that had been known and valued, as did the Germans, the French, the Belgians and the Dutch. And so we're still much more tied, even now, to conventional loyalties, to suspicions of other groups. And secondly, an important point I think, we can see that unity is not achieved by mere discussion. The vital impetus to unity comes from actual contact, from working together with people not of our own tradition.

Today, society even in England is, of course, being turned upside down and we all feel the effects. But the process is a gradual one now, and therefore it's easier for the timorous to escape its meaning by rationalizing or even blind bigotry. This will not do: the ground is shifting under our feet, and it's vital that we should face reality instead of trying to escape into a make-believe world of our own. The times *are* changing and a good thing too. The old barriers are breaking down; the challenge with which our times confront us is simply this: are we going to enter into the search for unity among men, or shall we deceive ourselves into thinking that nothing new is happening?—for we shall deceive only *ourselves*, and the world will pass us by.

The extension of Christ's kingdom throughout the world

A question that we should ask ourselves in thinking about the unity of Christians is just what we *mean* by 'the spread of Christ's kingdom'.

At least since the reformation, the Catholic attitude was largely based on the assumption that the kingdom of Christ exists already and is to be found among those in communion with the Bishop of Rome. On this assumption, the spread of the kingdom simply meant getting more and more people to come into that communion, without in any way adapting the nature of the Roman Church itself.

There are two major objections to this contention. First of all, the fundamental Christian experience of community in common purpose, of concern for others even to the point of self-sacrifice ('see how these Christians love each other'), is found among Christian groups outside the Roman communion; it is found, too, among groups who do not accept Christian dogma at all. Secondly, we do *not* always find it in the Roman communion (in fact, that's something of an understatement). Even at this day, the total self-giving in love which was Christ's vital contribution to human living is a rare thing, found only here and there, and not only in the Church. It just isn't possible to identify it with any particular organization or grouping.

Then what is the point of the Church? I think there is no doubt that the approach to life that we call 'Christian' really does spring from Christ himself. It seems too to be more common the more a society is influenced by the historical Christian tradition, and for persistent historical influence organized Christianity is essential; and the Church, centred on the pope, is undoubtedly organized Christianity. Without the living, communal *tradition* which springs from an organized Church it is impossible to envisage the growth of Christian insight in the world.

If we think about it, we Catholics find ourselves in a rather alarming position, as those responsible for the centre of the only vision that can redeem man from himself and from that self-centredness which threatens the future not only of individuals but of mankind as a whole. And yet we're not in any position either to explain, or, still less, to live out perfectly, what we stand for. And so we've failed, so far, to unite man into one whole.

But there's no reason to despair—rather the contrary. We don't expect the total unification of mankind except as the fulfilment of the creative act of God, which is going on now and of which we are part. The kingdom of God will be finally realized when creation is completed with what we call the Second Coming. Until then, we must continue to seek for the meaning in life that is implicit in our tradition. We must try, too, in common with others, to show it in our lives so that the great idea may live and spread throughout the world.

XVII

ON THE CHURCH

Who is the Church?

ST PAUL, thinking particularly of the exodus from Egypt and the crossing of the Red Sea, describes how all the Jews went through the same experiences: the baptism of passing through the Red Sea; the eating of the same food (the manna) and the drinking of the same drink. And yet, he says, 'with most of them God was not well pleased'.

St Paul obviously intended his readers to relate this to the Christian community. We are all baptized and we all receive the same food in the Eucharist—as St Paul says elsewhere 'We being many are one body because we all eat of the same bread.' And the same conclusion is to be inferred: with most of us God is not well pleased.

Now it is perfectly obvious, as we all know, that there are immense numbers of Christians who fail culpably to live up to what they profess. But there are also a great many who don't really see what Christianity is about at all: their religion means something to them which is not Christianity. This is not culpable, but it is certainly a problem. Likewise, there are many non-Christians who *do* see the vital thing about *living* that Christianity stands for, although they may not necessarily connect what they see with Christianity.

What bearing does all this have on our understanding of the doctrine of the Church? I want to try to outline a tentative answer to this question—but I admit that it is only tentative.

Judaism was not sectarian. You might think it was, because

it was limited to one exclusive group of people, but in a very important sense it was not sectarian: it was a *national* religion, not a group within a group. The whole body of the Jews belonged to the same community: and they did not distinguish between the religious and the political community. Judaism therefore included good Jews and bad Jews; those who were aware of what Judaism was about and those who were not. Within this all-inclusive community there was a central stream of insight which finds expression itself in the Old Testament, particularly in the writings of the prophets and the chroniclers, who saw a pattern in the course of Jewish history. These people *were* aware of a growth in Israel.

Now, Christianity is not sectarian either, but universal, Catholic. It involves all men. The effect of Christ's life was not to produce another closed group like the Jews with the only difference that it was international. The Christ-event broke open the old situation where there was a limited 'chosen people'; now the chosen people consists of the whole of mankind. It was no longer simply one nation that was seen to be involved, but all men. Some of the early Christian writers are insistent that Christianity involves all men, that there is a sense in which all men are in the Church.

We must see the Church as somehow comparable with that central stream of insight among the Jewish people in which we can see and trace, by the evidence of what they wrote, the development of their insight and understanding. We must see in the Church a community which necessarily has a certain organization; within it, a developing insight into the meaning of life and the significance of the whole world is growing. This view would seem to allow for those people who technically belong to the Church, the organized community, but who may not have insight; it allows too for a certain amount of give and take, as it were, as regards people who are not technically members of the Church and yet do have some insight into what life is about: for in so far as their insight is true, they do see what Christianity is about.

Sectarianism

It is interesting to notice how sectarian were the reactions of the Samaritan woman when she met Jesus. For instance, the very first thing she comments on is that Jesus, a Jew, had spoken to her, a Samaritan. And once she has been duly impressed by him and can accept him as an authority, the first question she asks is: 'Should we worship here in this mountain, or are the Jews right in saying men should worship at Jerusalem —who is right?' When the disciples come on the scene they show equally sectarian reactions.

Isn't all this remarkably like what goes on today? I often come across people of a different Christian tradition from our own, and whether they admire or despise or distrust the Catholic Church, the same question is clearly in their minds— *who* is right, the Catholic, the Anglican, the Methodist, the humanist? They feel one of these must be *right* and the others *wrong*.

Look again at Christ's answer to the Samaritan woman's question. Roughly translated it is this: 'The time is now coming—indeed it has come—when neither this mountain nor Jerusalem is the special place for prayer; the barriers are being destroyed and God is no longer to be seen as limited to any one place or to any one race or group of people.' Perhaps the failure to understand what this means is at the root of our confusion today, with all the mutual suspicion between Christians, and the non-Christian's suspicion of Christians.

We have let our religion become exclusive. Take, for example, the Eucharist—and it is in fact a central example. In the early Church the Eucharist was primarily a meal—a *real* meal, though one embodying certain ritual just as the Jewish passover feast had done, ending with the blessing of the bread and the cup. To the conventional religious mind of the day, this was quite unrecognizable as worship. However, over the centuries, we have increasingly tended to make it conform to the conventional religious idea of worship found both in Judaism and paganism, building special temples in which to celebrate it, surrounding it with ceremonial, and it has become less and less like a meal—the universal symbol of human unity—and more and more exclusive.

We should not forget that the word 'Catholic' means 'universal', not 'exclusive'.

Responsibility

Ezekiel lived and wrote about five hundred years before Christ, at a time when the Jewish people were undergoing considerable hardships. There had been a great deal of serious social unrest and social injustice in the past and the state had declined, become divided against itself, and was in his time under threat of total extinction at the hands of the Babylonians. He attacks, among other things, a particular line of thought which was evidently popular—the saying of the proverb 'the fathers have eaten sour grapes and the children's teeth are set on edge', which puts the blame for the present state of affairs not on ourselves but on our fathers and ancestors.

There is, of course, an element of truth in the proverb: nobody is *entirely* responsible for the situation in which he finds himself. This is true of communities and also of individuals. Obviously an individual's background, upbringing and so on do affect his responsibility, and for that the individual is not to be blamed. But Ezekiel is attacking the denial of all responsibility and the failure to attempt to alter things. It's a common human tendency, to blame other people, anyone but ourselves, for what is going wrong and to expect them to put it right: 'What are "they" going to do about it?'

So Ezekiel says quite clearly that God does not condemn men for what is not their fault, but that men *are* responsible. He doesn't deny that there are things for which individuals are not responsible: as a Jew he was fully aware of the responsibility of the whole people for the situation they were in. But he did attack the idea that the individual had no responsibility, and insisted that the *limited* responsibility which men have must be *fully* used.

It's worth noting what he lists as important: justice, feeding the hungry, clothing the naked: in short, having a concern for other people. There is one rather surprising omission in this list: he doesn't mention the worship of God in the temple as necessary. This—though it would have been taken for granted —is not what came to Ezekiel's mind when he was listing the things upon which a man will be judged. Many prophets before him had gone so far as to say that God does *not* want sacrifice, but that he *does* want justice, righteousness and humility.

Now Christ was a Jew and he claimed to fulfil the Jewish tradition. And the Jewish religion was not, for all that they had a temple and, later, synagogues, *centred* on a formalized attitude of worship of God. Its centre was the knowing of God in the informal but deep and true relationships between man and man in community—and *this* was what Christ fulfilled.

Yet even today we find many who seem to think that the acid test of Christianity is that people should take part in the Church's worship. It is not. The acid test of Christianity is to be found in the rather untidy and informal world in which man is united with man in love and service.

Like Ezekiel and the Jews, we should take it for granted that we worship and go to church; but this will mean *nothing* unless we have experienced, in the informality of human relation-
of the power will see the Mass appear as the formal ex-

pression of the ultimate, the unified purpose of which our own experience in our own human relationships is a part. It will be to them the manifestation of an awareness of what life as a whole is all about.

XVIII

THE MONASTIC LIFE:
SEARCH FOR COMMUNITY

WE MUST clear the ground by saying straight away that the point of monasticism is not asceticism; nor is it the singing of the Divine Office; nor even praying on behalf of others. None of these is the really central and significant thing that distinguishes the monastic life from others: the really central point is Community.

The monk takes a vow of stability which commits him to a local community, and to one that has the essentially organic quality of containing all age groups, the young representing the future. In this respect it's different from any other Order—Franciscan, Jesuit, Dominican and so on—whose members do not make a vow to belong to a particular community, but only to an order which is world-wide, and who may find themselves sent anywhere. The Benedictine commits himself to a particular local community. But of course the community is never perfect, and so the monk finds himself committed to *discovering* the meaning of true community.

The question could well be asked, 'But aren't we all committed to this by virtue of being Christians?'—to which the answer must be, 'Yes, we are.' But there is a difficulty here. The usual pattern of life is, of course, married life, and love in marriage at its best is the highest concentration, so to speak, of the experience of community found anywhere among men—it is the *highest* concentration, but it lacks universal applicability. What I mean is that not all human relationships can be worked out on the model of marriage and the love of a man for a woman; and further, love in marriage is highly localized and incommunicable except, in a sense, to the children. Yet it is necessary for man to seek the all-inclusive *society*, founded on the law of love and freedom, instead of that which we still know (with some mitigations) of fear and constraint in the individual.

There is no precedent for such a society. It has never been known, at any time in human history, and for this very reason a really strong faith that it can ever be achieved is needed to give us the impetus to strive for it. Even granted such faith, there's a tremendous nervous strain on those who commit themselves, without any escape route, to this search: one that penetrates to the very fibres of their being. There are few consolations in the search and there's much pain and anguish.

But for all this, we Christians do believe that the search is not in vain. It is a way of saying that we believe man to be redeemable. And, within the very complex pattern of human seeking, the monastic community above all is committed to the search.

XIX

AUTHORITY

The authority of Christ

THERE IS A PROBLEM running right through the Old Testament and presented very clearly in the New: the problem of authority; of the relationship between ruler and ruled.

The Old Testament is full of stories—some legendary, some historical—in which the younger supplants the older or the subject supplants the ruler: think of Jacob and Esau, of Joseph and his family, of Moses and Pharoah, of Samuel and Eli, David and Saul. In the New Testament we see this taken rather further, in remarks like St Paul's: 'God has chosen the weak things of the earth [those who are not in power, not in authority as we normally mean the word] to confound the strong.'

Our Lord's teaching returns constantly to this theme. The stone which the builders rejected becomes the head of the corner. He constantly accuses the Scribes and Pharisees of being blind leaders of the blind: leaders, 'in authority', but completely closed to any new insight. His life teaches us the same thing. His credentials were poor for one who was supposed to be a teacher; he was not a Pharisee, he was not of the teaching or ruling class, he was untrained—and yet he 'spoke with authority, and not as the Scribes'. He spoke with a tremendous conviction and in such a way that people, hearing him, believed him—a thing they did not experience with the Scribes. Yet he refused to replace, to supplant, to make himself an authority in the way that the scribes and Pharisees were; he refused to have any truck at all with a messianic rising. And because of this refusal to assume this kind of leadership, it was undoubtedly easier for his enemies to do away with him.

Well, the implications of all this are too many to be discussed here. But it is surely clear that our society, whether we are talking about the political or the ecclesiastical set-up, does not share Christ's approach to authority. We talk of those in authority as being 'in power'—a very significant phrase; and those in power spend their time building up *defences* against those who disagree with them, instead of seeking to learn from them. Parties are formed, factions dispute with each other. In fact, such authorities resemble too closely for comfort the wicked husbandmen who failed to produce the fruits of the vine entrusted to them. And unfortunately, but perhaps understandably in the circumstances, the opposition share the same faults—seeking to obtain power (the very thing our Lord refused to do), to overthrow the existing regime and to take its place. All too easily we men, in whatever we try to achieve in common, tend to adopt the political mentality that produces opposition rather than cooperation. We should not forget another saying of our Lord's: 'A kingdom divided against itself cannot stand.'

Leadership: the question of James and John

After James and John—or their mother, according to one evangelist—ask to be given the places of highest rank in the kingdom, Christ speaks about rank in society. He mentions the 'rulers of the Gentiles' who 'lord it over' their subjects—and points out that this idea of rank is completely out of the question for those who follow him. He does not say that the Gentiles fail to rule well, and that Christians must do better. No, broadly speaking the rulers of the Gentiles manage quite well, but their *way* is rejected by Christ as being *less mature,* not of his kingdom. What he is saying is that the kind of leadership that is more responsible, more adult, is where the leader serves the people. Only with this kind of leadership can the Christian vision of peace and unity among men possibly be realized.

We cannot deny, I think, that the Church which goes under the name of Christian has often presented an extremely poor example of such leadership, constantly imitating the structures of authority in the society of its time—popes and bishops have behaved like kings and great lords, not only in the pomp with which they have surrounded themselves, but also in their authoritarian attitude to those under their care. In other words, the Church always tends to stay at the level of immaturity of the world in which it is operating—and the consequence of this is to perpetuate immaturity and irresponsibility in its members, both in the leaders and in those led.

Grace and all that: those subject to us

In one of the Sunday collects[1] we ask God to see 'that we put not our trust in anything that we do'. We might misunderstand this, and say that we are capable of nothing. But this would make all human effort, all attempt to *achieve* anything in this life, futile, and would contradict the central point of Christianity in the incarnation.

Let's look at the phrase from a different angle. You sometimes hear schoolmasters (and not only schoolmasters) talking of moulding people's characters, 'moulding the characters of the young'. And the image behind this in their minds is that the child starts off as a sort of blank sheet of paper, on which the master can draw whatever he chooses. He can *direct* the pattern

[1]Sexagesima Sunday.

of growth, and by saying the right things at the right time or by putting the child through the right sort of processes, get a character in a particular mould according to the plan of the educator.

Now this is the mentality not only of some schoolmasters but also of parents and other authorities, both in state and Church. (Incidentally, also, sometimes it shows in our attitude to ourselves, when we try to make ourselves fit a certain preconceived character which suits our own picture of ourselves.)

Yet it is an attitude bitterly resented—and quite rightly so—by the more aware of those who are supposed to be being moulded. The protest is often incoherent, though occasionally it comes out loud and clear—even from boys at school. What is wrong with it? Well, it seems to me that such an attitude denies three things.

First it denies that each man or woman is a new creation in process of being created: it tries to override this and to fashion him according to a blueprint in the mind of the educator—whether he be schoolmaster, parent, or authority in Church or state. Secondly, it denies the activity of the Holy Spirit: the Holy Spirit who, as our Lord said, 'blows where he will'. We don't know where he comes from or where he goes: we cannot pin-point the Spirit. We must have faith in the growth of the world according to God's creative Spirit. And thirdly, it denies grace or the *spontaneity* of growth by trying to channel it along certain preconceived routes.

So when we pray that we 'put not our trust in anything that we do' we should not mean to abstain from achievement; nor on the other hand should we try to channel and limit what may be achieved along our own preselected railway lines, whether they are designed for ourselves or for anyone else.

The activity of the Spirit

Perhaps one of the most dangerous errors common in Christian parlance is to say that God *created* the world—in the past tense. Because as soon as you can use the past tense you relegate creation to a mere story of origin, over and done with, and enter into the atmosphere of the fairy story. What we must see is that nothing is created in a moment of time, at a snap of God's fingers: the growth of a thing is an integral part of its creation.

This is true of the universe as a whole—the story of evolution is the story of a creation still far from completed. It's true of all human communities and of the whole world-wide human community. It is the key to understanding the Old Testament, where we have written evidence of a people in process of creation, developing as they 'grow up' a deeper understanding of the meaning of life. It's also the key to understanding the history of mankind, particularly after the culmination of Jewish growth in Christ, and it is the key to understanding the development of Christian doctrine which we say is always the same and yet always developing—just as we know ourselves individually to be always developing and yet remaining the same person.

It is in the very nature of growth that it cannot be *controlled*, but only arrested or stunted. If we have too clear a picture of what we *are* individually, or what man *is*, or of what the Church *is* or of what the universe *is* or what God *is*, and try to force growth according to that picture, all we succeed in doing is to arrest our own development and to fossilize ourselves.

We shall not wholly succeed in fossilizing others, however (though some of our efforts seem fairly successful), as the edu-

cator who thinks in terms of 'moulding characters' ought to find
out sooner or later. The creative Spirit of God cannot be
smothered. But we shall undoubtedly fossilize *ourselves* if we
persist in this attitude.

'We do not know,' says St John, 'what we shall be', but we
must remain open to growth—open to the free gift that is
grace. 'Ask and you shall receive; seek and you shall find; knock
and it shall be opened to you.'

Rules, and growth into Christ

We tend to think in terms of moral opposites: the 'good'
life and the 'bad' life. So we try to find a system of rules by
which we may live and which will reassure us that we are
living the 'good' life. We expect this system to be set up by the
Church, who will provide clear instructions as to the 'good'
things to do for all occasions.

There is something terribly unsatisfactory about this, because
it leads to a demand for the wrong kind of authority: authority
which would prevent us from having to think for ourselves and
would provide a *substitute* for our own conscience—a false
substitute, as it is bound to be, depriving us of any moral sense
of our own. With this outlook we tend to feel that if we can
'get around' the law without breaking it, there is nothing with
which we need reproach ourselves.

I suggest that we should not be thinking in terms of the
'good' and the 'bad' life at all. For a start probably no individual
lives either—we all fall somewhere between the two extremes.
We need to give more attention to *growth*. All of us were
born selfish. We don't blame a *child* for being self-centred,
because it is of the nature of human life that we should start so.
But we do complain if an adult is self-centred, and we rightly

associate self-centredness in an adult with childishness: which of course means that we are all childish to some extent (if we can't see that, there's not much hope for us).

St Paul talks about the need for man to grow in *maturity* towards fulfilment in Christ. To give one example from his writings: a Christian, he says, should know how to marry in holiness and not in lust—in self-giving instead of for his selfish satisfaction, 'for God has not called us for uncleanness, but to holiness'. This is not a question of obeying rules laid down by a society: holiness differs from uncleanness (and not of course only in sexual matters) as maturity differs from childishness, love from selfishness, giving from taking.

XX

GIVING OURSELVES

What else have we?

ST PAUL tells the Romans to 'owe nothing to anyone—except love'. If he had not added the bit about love, this would sound like an exhortation to behave in exactly the reverse of a Christian way—to owe nothing to anyone, to keep yourself to yourself and all the rest of it. But he says 'except to love one another', and adds that if we do *that*, then we have fulfilled the law. In fact of course love is more positive than that: by loving one another, we do more than fulfil the law. Look at the demands of the law, and try to imagine a world in which everyone did these things *and no more*: did *not* speak or behave uncharitably; did *not* steal or be dishonest; did *not* commit adultery. A world in which no one did any of these things, but did nothing positive either, would be dull and boring—and quite incapable of progress. To love, on the other hand, is to give ourselves completely, to do the things no one could make laws for and which are yet the things that bring light into the world—and in this love, in this total self-giving, we discover our real selves.

Giving ourselves. What else, when you think about it, *is* there for us to give? Anything other than ourselves becomes a kind of *payment* which eases our conscience, gives a certain limited satisfaction while we continue to keep ourselves to ourselves. If we are only giving *things* that are ours we still remain separate, an island jealously guarded. And we remain uncommitted observers—bystanders in the flow of life.

Remember how, after the storm on the lake in which the

disciples had shown fear, Jesus asks them, 'Why are you fearful, O ye of little faith?' Fear and faith are opposites: fear is what holds us back from self-giving, because we are sure of so little; we fear rejection perhaps, but we also fear that in giving ourselves we may lose ourselves. Faith, on the other hand, is fearlessness in the face of life and the future, and is based on a confidence born of limited experience by which we found that our greatest joy came when we had seemingly forgotten ourselves.

You may be wondering where God comes into all this. Well, we've really been talking about him all the time, because it is precisely in giving ourselves to others that we come to know God. If, on the contrary, we try to withdraw from others, thinking we can 'turn' elsewhere to God, we shall end up by chasing an illusion, a god who does not in fact exist at all.

On the 'two loves'

The other day I was talking to someone who was making the rather drastic and searching criticism of his attitude to life that we should all make from time to time. He said that he felt worried not so much by any special wrong act—sin—but just by a sense that he 'failed to give himself to others and to God'. Now it is clearly an important step to get beyond thinking just in terms of 'Have I broken the law or not?' to an awareness of a general and seemingly insoluble inadequacy about one's life, even if there are no 'mortal sins'; but what I want to examine is a still more fundamental problem that is hidden in the way this person expressed himself.

What I mean is that we ought not to be thinking about giving ourselves to people on the *one* hand, and to God on the *other* hand. St John writes, 'Whoever is unjust or does not love his

brother *is not of God.*' Love of God *is* love of others, and
there's no way to God except through others. As St John says
elsewhere, 'The man who says he loves God and does not love
his brother is a liar.' Taking this idea further, he says, 'We
know that we have passed from death to life, because we love
the brethren.' Passing from the nothingness of death, in which
we find ourselves when we realize that we are living in an isolation of our own, we come to know the resurrection when we
pass out of this isolation into an attitude in which we find
ourselves living for others. 'The man who does *not* love remains
in death'—remains in the meaninglessness of himself as an
isolated individual.

Now it is clear that for St John, and for all who truly begin
to see what the Christian thing is really about, there is only
one love, only one giving of ourselves—to other people, in
whom we find that we have in fact given ourselves to God.
What is also clear is that this process cannot possibly be ex-
plained by a purely rational process: the man who has not been
psychologically changed by the explosive attitude of Christ to
the world will say *either* (if he's humanistically minded) that if
we love others there's no need to bring in God, *or* (if he's 're-
ligiously' minded) that we must love others, but *also*—and
above all—we must love God. *Both* these attitudes miss the
point, which is the point of the incarnation—for men, God is
known *in* men (so Christ was God-in-man and man-in-God);
and love of others transcends the other, goes beyond him to
have an eternal value.

Finally, St John says, 'He laid down his life for us; and we
ought to lay down our lives for the brethren.' Not all can be
martyrs in the technical sense, but that is not the point. What
is the point is that a true love of others means a constant and
real death which is consummated by, and alone makes sense of,
our final physical death.

XXI

ON BLINDNESS

THE STORY OF THE healing of the blind man in John's gospel is more than a study in physical blindness. The man who had been blind was cured; but the main interest of the story is the blindness that remained uncured, the blindness of the Pharisees who refused to accept what had happened. They said: that for one thing the healer was a sinner, he'd cured on the Sabbath day, so he had no respect for the law; then, he had no credentials; they didn't recognize his ancestry or place of origin as significant because they didn't fit the prophecies. The cured man simply states the facts as he knew them: 'I was blind and now I see—this is all I know—and this seems to me to be a sign of the goodness of the man who did it.' And all they can answer to that is: 'You were born in sin, and you have the cheek to try to teach us. We know the answer, and it couldn't have happened.' The Pharisees stubbornly held to their theory, their preconceived notions, and refused to accept the observed fact.

We human beings seem to have a profound fear of truth when it undermines our most treasured prejudices, because then it seems to attack the whole basis on which we have built our lives. We can see this in most fields of activity, but in particular in politics and ecclesiastical allegiance, because these things provide the principles on which people build their lives. And so when people are faced with a fact that doesn't fit the pattern they have imposed on the world, and are basing their lives on, they become irrational, bigoted, uncharitable, and it is impossible to discuss anything with them.

We had an example of this in 1966 when Archbishop Ramsey's visit to the Pope excited a reaction from those two charming Northern Irish Presbyterian ministers which was so gloriously out of date (about four hundred years), based entirely on completely blind presuppositions as to what Roman Catholicism is all about, what the Pope would say, what the Archbishop was trying to do. The whole visit was seen as a contravention of an Elizabethan statute which declared it high treason to have anything to do with the Court of Rome. We find this an extraordinary attitude. Yet it is a sign of this very same blindness I have been talking about: there is nothing more disconcerting than to face challenge, any evidence that seems to undermine what you have based your life on. And of course, this blindness isn't limited to Northern Irish clergymen; nor is it limited to Protestants. It's found just as much among Catholics: the same fear, the same prejudice, the same refusal to accept the truth about the goodness and the achievements and the worthwhileness of good people who don't happen to be Roman Catholics.

All this is totally alien to the outlook of Christ. The political and ecclesiastical pushing and shoving that we see going on creates artificial barriers between men. The whole point of the movement that stems from Christ is that such barriers are to be destroyed, and that truth and love are all that matters—even if sometimes they're uncomfortable and inconvenient.

XXII

TO BE 'OF GOD'

WE READ IN St John's gospel: 'He that is of God hears the words of God. Therefore *you* do not hear them because you are not of God.' The people Jesus is speaking to were those who accepted the orthodox Jewish interpretation of the law and the requirements of the law. And this sort of language was clearly infuriating to such people, whose whole life was based on a careful observance of the law as they understood it, often at a considerable effort to themselves. It's as though someone were to get up and say to a group of clergy and what we please to call 'good Catholic laymen' that they are not of God, and so haven't the ghost of a notion what Christianity is all about: the audience would be horrified and angry. What did Christ mean by being 'of God', if people who gave so much consideration and effort to the service of God in the Law were not of God ?

We need to ask first what he did not mean. The conventionally religious man slips into thinking that to be 'of God' (or, to use the old-fashioned word one doesn't hear nowadays, 'godly') is to observe the rules well. The good Catholic, then, would be the one who goes to Mass every Sunday and, perhaps more often, who is honest in business, lives a good family life, doesn't do any harm to anyone and contributes as required to the needs of the Church. But the trouble is that people who live like this tend to become complacent, losing all sense of their own need. They cease to have, if ever they had, an openness to change and growth and new ideas, or a sense of community which would make them feel as responsible as anyone else for the failures of the society in which they live. They don't admit this responsibility because they are satisfied that their way of life is adequate: they are good Catholics. And so they fall into living out an unproductive routine.

This was the kind of person Christ accused of being 'not of God'. We need to face this fact, try to understand it, and not to be afraid of it. And, in contrast, those who were 'of God' turned out to be like the sinful woman who anointed Jesus's feet in the house of Simon the Pharisee—just the kind of person who was most despised (or, at the best, least respected) by the good-living routine-ridden people of her day.

It isn't easy to point the moral here. But surely we can say this: while we don't need to be in 'grave sin' to understand what Christ is talking about, we do need to know ourselves to be inadequate—as grave sinners are likely to do—so that we can be open to new possibilities, new ideas, and above all the need for growth, for our own growth and development, for the deepening of our understanding and the improvement of the way we live. And then we shall seek enlightenment and improvement of ourselves and the society we live in, and shan't be bogged down by self-satisfaction.

XXIII

GIVING THE GLORY TO GOD

' "LET HIM WHO BOASTS, BOAST IN THE LORD", for it is not the man who commends himself that is accepted, but the man whom the Lord commends.'

There is a great problem about humility, 'giving the glory to God' and so on, and it is not restricted to priests, monks and nuns, as spiritual books sometimes suggest: how, for instance, can the successful architect, surgeon, salesman, office-manager or schoolmaster give the glory (i.e., the credit) for his achievement to God? It is not sufficient to say that our gifts are inborn and so not self-given (although this is obviously true); we still know that it depends on *us* whether we use these gifts at all and if so whether we use them constructively in the service of mankind.

The real difficulty, I think, lies in our notion of God to whom, we say, glory for our achievements should be given. Most people either *believe in* or *reject* a *mechanistic* idea of God, a 'God-outside' who created and occasionally intervenes in his creation, or an 'explanation-God' who is produced as filling up the gaps in our knowledge about the world. At the best, this sort of God can only be given the credit for the crude material of our lives, our latent abilities and so on, and not for the way in which we develop them nor for what we achieve with them.

In fact such an idea of God is badly wrong: this is not a God we know by experience, but only the product of a process of speculative thought. God is the source and goal of life, and we know him in our experience, in our commitment to things, and to projects, and above all to people, which is what goes to build up the world. It is in our activity that God is *discovered*, and the truth is that whatever our initial gifts, if we don't seek to achieve we shall never know God at all.

All achievement in this world is the achievement of God, in two senses. First, there is the achievement of the creative Spirit in which our own spirits take part *because they are part of it themselves*; and secondly, God is actually achieved by us and in us in creative living. In one single creative process (an 'act', yes, but one that is still going on) God *achieves* and *is achieved by* man. This is the meaning of the incarnation—for in Christ not only did God become man, but in one and the same event man became God.